TWO SONS AND A FATHER

YOUR FATHER, YOUR INHERITANCE

DALE L. MAST

Table of Contents

Introduction

There are many themes and truths in the parable that Jesus taught known as *The Prodigal Son*. Some have titled it, *The Loving Father*.

Jesus, the one unique Son, was telling this parable for those listening to gain a better understanding of His Father. Religious leaders were upset with Jesus because of the friendships He was building. These relationships were with people not approved of by the religious leaders. Jesus used three parables to help them understand His Father's love for all of humanity.

The parable we will be studying deals with two sons, a father, and their inheritance. It was taught by Jesus to give us insight into our heart. The way we approach Father God for our inheritance reveals our relationship with Him. There are keys to our inheritance that Jesus taught in this parable that will increase our ability to reach our destiny.

We must come to an understanding that God is our Father. That makes us "sons." Sons receive an inheritance. Our inheritance will be wasted without His presence. If we cannot access our inheritance, we've not learned how to relate to our Father as a son.

As we read the parable, the selfishness and rebellion of the prodigal son who immediately left his father after receiving his inheritance is quite obvious. The older son remained with his father. We must be careful that we do not confuse the older son's work ethic as faithfulness to his father. He was obviously faithful to his duties, yet quite distant from his father.

The older son was much more comfortable working in his father's fields than being in his father's presence — like many believers. If we truly enjoy His presence, Father God works through us. This is not just a play on words, but a world of difference.

The prodigal son did not *want* to live in his father's presence. The older son did not know *how* to live in his father's presence. Neither son desired the father. Each son was focused on his inheritance — overlooking their father.

The closer we draw to Father God, the more we will understand Him and ourselves. An intimate friendship with our Father causes His greatness to naturally flow through our lives — bringing glory and honor to Him. Until we are absolutely amazed by what we do, we have not yet tapped into the greatness of our Father God. Move closer to your Father. Expect more.

If a father can sing, we expect the son to have the same ability. Our Father God is full of wisdom, strength, and abilities that he fully poured into His Only Begotten Son. He has also given us His gifts and His anointing to each of us—but not all to any of us. Our Father's greatness flows through us by His Spirit.

It is His pleasure to give *us* the kingdom. That is why our unity brings a stronger anointing. The abilities of the Father were manifested in His Only Son and He will continue to show His greatness through every son in unique ways!

If the entire Body Of Christ were squeezed together into one—we would be a very complete representation of our Father's anointing and character—as we remain connected to the Head—*Jesus*. There is a reason we are called the *Body of Christ*.

Privileged Sons

Many people refer to Father God as "the man upstairs." It most likely was born from a broken relationship with their natural father. He provided for them, but they never really knew him—nor did he know them. A meaningful relationship was simply out of the question. He would show up now and then to help them—and then return to what he was really interested in doing. He was "the man," never the father.

The number-one attack of the enemy is to block our ability to see God as our Father—and ourselves as privileged sons.

When the disciples asked Jesus to teach them how to pray, the first two words He gave them were, "Our Father," and these set the tone and reality of the entire prayer. If these two words do not grip our hearts, the rest of the words in the Lord's Prayer lose context, as well as the implicit favor that comes from that dynamic personal relationship. Go deeper.

If you entered a bank to receive a loan, the application process would be shortened, if not totally disregarded, if your father were the owner and president of the bank. You would not be subject to all the guidelines and requirements set for others, because you would have exceeded them—not neglected them.

You would no longer be waiting your turn as an ordinary customer to talk with a loan officer—as soon as you informed the new employee that you were the son of the bank owner and president. Your spirit, mannerisms, and physical resemblance to your father would be the first indicator to anyone who was otherwise uninformed. It must be accompanied by your confident assertion with a voice that reminds them of his. The love and respect emanating from your heart and your every gesture would ease their slightest uncertainties.

As soon as it was verified, you would immediately be ushered into the president's office—unless you temporarily forgot that he was your father. Then you would come as an ordinary customer, instead of a son—but you are a son!

The loan would now be based on the fact that you are his son, and your specific request and purpose, subject only to your father's wisdom. It would be limited by his net worth—not your ability to pay back the loan.

As Christians, it is easy for us to comprehend that we are God's children, because we view our salvation like our spiritual birthday. We experience numerous birthday celebrations with gifts given and received every year, so it is easy for us expect blessings now and then from God.

An inheritance occurs only once or twice in our entire life. Some of us never experience it. Therefore it is difficult for us to think in terms of an inheritance as we view our journey and destiny. We become content with blessings, limiting our future.

If we do not see God as our Father we will not even expect an inheritance or factor in that huge advantage as we approach Father God with a specific request concerning our life needs.

Our natural fathers could only help us navigate through some of our life challenges, but not all of them—and for some people, none of them as their relationship with their father was hurtful or absent.

Even the best father still falls short of Father God, but they are a huge advantage in teaching us how approach "Our Father." Great fathers create a healthy mindset and positive expectations in their children concerning Father God.

The role of a natural father ultimately, is to link his children to Father God. The enemy knows this and he fights to destroy this pivotal relationship.

My wife, LuAnne, has great faith that what she asks Father God she will receive. It is easy for her, because her father always tried to get for her what she wanted. I encourage you to read her book, *God, I Feel like Cinderella!*

Most believers have a great connection with Jesus, as He is the central figure communicated to bring us to salvation. The Father is often portrayed as the stern judge, with loving Jesus intervening for our salvation.

Our view of the Father is often warped from the first day of our new birth. God so loved the world that He sent His Son. The Father's love for us is what moved Jesus to come to earth. Take another look at Our Father. It has taken years for the church to embrace Father God, but now it has become a leading truth for wholeness and authority.

There are many hurts in life with *fathers*—people in authority. We tend to approach God more like an all-powerful detached banker, instead of *our father* who owns the bank and truly desires to meet our life goals and desires. We come to Him seeking a blessing—not our inheritance. There's nothing wrong with that, it's just limited.

We often list our accomplishments and solid track record to impress Him—trying to break the reluctance we have projected on Him to have our requests granted. The enemy has blocked our ability to see the entire favor we already have. The application for approval focuses on our faithful labor over time to gain a corresponding blessing like an employee seeking a bonus or a raise.

We are not coming as a son, expecting an inheritance. We are coming as an employee desiring a blessing. We will normally receive what we believe, not what we need.

Faith in Our Father and His goodness, instead of our goodness, opens up endless possibilities. His goodness allows my faith to take flight, expecting the impossible. The focus of our faith and who we are to Him is a critical issue.

If we were standing among thousands of people to see a man of great importance, the status of anyone around us would not exceed our rank if we were his son. We could have the privilege of seeing him first.

A vice-president of a multi-billion dollar corporation does not have same access to the assets of the corporation as the president/owner. The son can never expect to earn the paycheck of the vice-president, yet the vice-president can never expect to receive the inheritance of the president's son. Being a son is more important than being important. Our inheritance would be a great point of interest—if we knew our father was wealthy. The riches of His glory are about to flood your life.

There is one critical key that cannot be overlooked concerning us as sons—we cannot address the president as others—he is not Mr. President to us—He is Father. Any title other than "Father" would reveal problems in our relationship. It would be offensive to any father. Father God does not like it any better. Get more comfortable calling Him—*Father.* He enjoys it.

When we approach Father God as a stranger, it is an affront to Him and how He desires to relate to us as His children. When our needs and visions are presented as from a son, it is the fulfillment of His purpose for mankind. Many requests He would grant are denied, simply because we ask as strangers—a relationship that is diametrically opposed to the very purpose of the cross of Jesus Christ.

Heaven and Earth is the Father, and the Son, and sons' business. Father God will not operate from any other paradigm with His children—it simply is not possible.

The primary purpose of Jesus dying on the cross was to restore our relationship to Father God, not to meet our needs. When that relationship is restored, our inheritance is set. He is more than your God—He is your Father!

Do not call anyone on earth your father; for One is your Father, He who is in heaven. [1]

We often debate if we should call any man father—and forget to call the One who is our Father—Father. All through the scriptures it refers to fathers and sons, so that's not the point. Start using the word Father when talking to Him.

I am a man, married to my wife. She does not call me *man*. I am her husband. She does not call me *husband* when she is speaking to me. My name is Dale, but she most often calls me *baby*. You may not call me *baby*. When she does, it denotes the intimacy and covenant that we share. Anything less would downgrade our personal relationship.

Do not fear, little flock, for it is your Father's good pleasure to give you the kingdom. [2]

Jesus cannot lie—God is your Father! He is the Everlasting Father—The Eternal Father—He will never stop being your

---

[1] *The New King James Version*. (1982). (Mt 23:9). Nashville: Thomas Nelson.

[2] *The New King James Version*. (1982). (Lk 12:32). Nashville: Thomas Nelson.

Father. He will be your Father in Heaven. He is your Father on earth. He is your Father forever.

This causes us to "fear not." The enemy attempts to make us fear our Father to keep us from Him and our inheritance. It is our Father's love for us that dismantles that fear and releases the Kingdom to us with pleasure.

The fear of a child is broken when the strength and the love of the father is for them. We may see ourselves as a "little flock," but it is still our Father's pleasure to give the kingdom to us.

Pleasure is a word that denotes enjoyment and satisfaction that is embedded in the loving and generous attitude of our Father towards us, His sons. Our faith may have limits, but our relationship as a son gives us privileged access to who He is and what He has. He experiences more pleasure giving us His kingdom than we have receiving it.

His Kingdom and everything in it must be received as a son. It can never be earned or achieved. He does, however, require his sons to have a *priority and passion* for Him. It protects us from making our inheritance the focus of our heart—an idol.

Priority, passion, and His purposes work His purity in us. They are defining qualities of His sons that have access to their inheritance. Those same qualities live in our Father towards us. We have priority in His heart; He is passionate about us; and He pursues His purpose towards us that we might live in Him.

But seek first the kingdom of God and His righteousness, and all these things shall be added to you.[3]

All things include everything you'll ever need or desire in life that brings fulfillment and joy! Jesus said the kingdom of God was now at hand and that it actually exists within us. When we live in His presence, we become one with Him. When The Father dwells in His sons and daughters—there His Kingdom flourishes! Jesus lived in this dimension in His Father—a life of priority, passion and purpose that shifted the earth. Jesus calls us, "Follow Me."

Adam—A Son

Jesus was not the first creation of God the Father, but was actually God the Son—with God the Father—from the beginning of eternity. Jesus—who was, who is, and who is to come, had no beginning. That's just another way of saying our Father's name, "I Am." These are wonderful truths that we cannot fully explain, but we can easily understand.

God the Father and God the Son have opened up their circle, inviting us to relate as sons. Amazing! We are not coming to Father God as manservants or as angelic beings, but as His sons! Let the celebration and revelation begin!

Jesus became a perfect sacrifice to take away our sins. Yet there was more on the mind of our Father God than just

---

[3] *The New King James Version*. (1982). (Mt 6:33). Nashville: Thomas Nelson.

forgiveness. He used His only unique eternal God Son to restore our sonship that Adam lost. That is one of the reasons that Jesus is called the last Adam.

Our covenant and blessing is rooted in Abraham, the father of faith, but our purpose and assignment is found in Adam. Adam was a *covenant breaker* and Abraham was a *covenant maker*. We are, therefore, named the seed of Abraham. Abraham existed before Israel or the Church and he birthed both by his faith. When Abraham looked at the stars that night, he saw Israel and the Church. Fathers birth the will of God.

The life of the first man—Adam, and the last Adam—Jesus, unfold the revelation of our sonship to Father God. Why do you think we are seated in heavenly places in Christ Jesus? The seat at the right hand of Father God is an honored placed reserved exclusively for His "sons." Angels will never be allowed to be seated there. Let the honor of that seat begin to overwhelm us.

Jesus Christ, The Father's Only Begotten Son, paid the price to seat us next to our Father in heavenly places—while still on earth! Jesus came to earth to restore our chair in the Father's presence. Every child of God, enjoys His presence in that seat, but a son is a child of God who knows how to let his Father rule through him. A child and a son will always enjoy their Father's presence in that chair—but only a son can embrace his purpose from The Father's throne.

It is very important to understand these truths before we go into the story of the prodigal son for us to comprehend the entire scope Father God desires to restore to us. Adam was the genius of Father God, created as a son—in His likeness and image—and so were you! God created Adam and birthed him as He breathed His life into him. Adam and Eve had no belly button. God was their Father.

They enjoyed His presence every day before the fall. We were designed by God, so He could fit into us and we could fit into Him—in a unique father-son-daughter relationship.

Christ in you, the hope of glory.[4] He who abides in Me, and I in him, bears much fruit.[5] For in Him we live and move and have our being.[6]

If I were God, I would not have designed my subjects for that type of relationship. We are not subjects, we are sons and daughters! Aren't you glad I'm not God! I am glad you're not either.

We are the desire of The Father's heart. Father God created Adam's life on earth to function as a son to Him. Our Father has never shifted that pattern concerning mankind—pursuing the same relationship with mankind in every age.

---

[4] *The New King James Version*. (1982). (Col 1:27). Nashville: Thomas Nelson.

[5] *The New King James Version*. (1982). (Jn 15:5). Nashville: Thomas Nelson.

[6] *The New King James Version*. (1982). (Ac 17:28). Nashville: Thomas Nelson.

Your Inheritance

The story of the prodigal is also a study concerning inheritance. We must gain a greater understanding about it from Father God's perspective to appreciate the truths contained in this parable.

An inheritance is comprised of what someone possesses at the time of their death, willed to those still living. Because Jesus was God's Son and the last Adam, He could restore us as sons. What He possessed in his life at the time of His death— He has willed to us as our inheritance. Jesus possessed miracles, wisdom, and anointing at the time of His death; but there was much more He obtained in His life and death.

We see the cross as the place where Jesus loved us and paid the terrible price for our sins. That is very true. There is another truth we must not overlook when we consider the cross. The cross was an assignment of obedience that displayed the love and trust between The Son and His Father— in a painful dark void.

The cross was set upon the depth of the intimate relationship that existed between The Father and The Son of the universe. Golgotha was the arena where The Son preferred His Father's will above His personal desire—honoring His Father. The depth of that friendship and trust with The Father Jesus willed to us at His death.

The Tree of Life hung on the Tree of the Knowledge of Good and Evil to restore the relationship Adam and Eve lost with their Father. Their intimate fellowship with Father God was shattered, but not beyond repair.

We have all been trained in the knowledge of good and evil by this world and good religious people. Good people can despise the evil, yet never taste the fruit from the Tree of Life.

The first Adam lost his relationship with Father God in the Garden of Eden and was driven out of it. Angels guarded the entrance to keep out mankind. After Noah's flood, the Garden of Eden was decimated.

I believe, along with others, that Jerusalem was the original site of the Garden of Eden where the first Adam lost his intimate relationship with his Father. It would not surprise me if the cross of Jesus Christ was raised over the root system of the Tree of Life in the Garden of Eden—as He is still the Tree of Life today. Father God is into geography. Specific events are coordinated by Him to occur in specific locations and times to communicate truth to us in a strategic prophetic manner.

Jesus was born in Bethlehem in the lineage of David, but his assignment was in Jerusalem—the City of David— the decimated Garden of Eden. When Jesus returns, He will enter in through the Eastern Gate of Jerusalem to sit on the Throne of David. The last Adam will rule where the first Adam didn't—completing what Father God desired from the beginning. Sons complete what their Father desires.

Inheritance Restrictions

Now I say that the heir, as long as he is a child,
does not differ at all from a slave, though he
is master of all, but is under guardians and
stewards until the time appointed by the
father.[7] *(Gal. 4:1–2)*

A child is always a son, but a son is no longer a child. Until we become of age spiritually—as a son—we do not have full access to our inheritance. When we become children of God, we are no better off than slaves concerning our inheritance. We own it all—but we have limited access to it.

If a baby boy's wealthy parents died, he would be provided for out of his inheritance they willed to him. The child would not have personal access and authority to use it as he saw fit until he reached the mature age set by his parents or the laws of the land. There are spiritual laws concerning our inheritance in the heavenly realms that are set by our Father. They are multi-dimensional, but can only be accessed by sons of proper age. Our spiritual inheritance is *not* Heaven, nor is it reserved until we reach Heaven. That belief cancels our ability to receive it on the earth for the life we are now living.

It is impossible to reach *our destiny* on this earth without accessing *our inheritance.* Many Christians are "slaving

---

[7] *The New King James Version.* (1982). (Ga 4:1–2). Nashville: Thomas Nelson.

away" because they refuse to come to Father God for their inheritance. This is an acceptable form of rebellion for many believers—we call it "being responsible." The fallacy is our point of focus. We are looking at ourselves, thinking of what we have accomplished, instead of looking at Him who accomplished all of these things for us, then in us and through us.

If we are a child of God, we are granted the right to go from earth to Heaven at our death. If we are a "son" of God, we are granted the right to bring Heaven to earth with our life. Our Father God desires that His Kingdom be brought to earth by His sons, not by His angels.

Father God declared at the baptism of Jesus, "You are My Son whom I love; in you I am well pleased!" Our righteous obedience—love deeds of commitment—brings pleasure to Our Father—releasing the presence of the Holy Spirit. Receiving His pleasure is required to defeat the enemy in the wilderness so that we can live in the fullness of God's power.

Children are lovingly provided for by their father who meets their every need—while they are maturing. Sons have access to their inheritance for kingdom destiny assignments and blessings. Children have faith—sons are given authority.

Many believers are like a "child heir," which is the same as slaves concerning their inheritance. They are master of all, but still under guardians and stewards. Many Christians think they are living out of their full inheritance, yet they are still under guardians and stewards with limited access—while still experiencing more than most believers. What would our lives look like if we gained full access to our inheritance with a mature view of our life—and Our Father?

The maturity of our relationship to Father God and our appointed time give us access to our inheritance. The maturity will not allow us to abuse it, misuse it or forget it. The *stuff* of our inheritance can be gained by request as a son, but without the Father's presence we have not obtained a true inheritance. The *who* is greater than the *what*.

Someone must die for you to receive an inheritance. Jesus did. Would you please claim and utilize what Jesus died and willed to you? You must come as a privileged son to claim your inheritance, not a sinner saved by grace—but don't ever forget that you were.

We must shift our identity from the description of our salvation—to the purpose of our salvation. We must shift our identity from the event that brought us life, to the life we are now living in Christ Jesus. We cannot be defined by who we were as we came through the door, but rather by the seat of honor that we now enjoy.

We don't need our inheritance in Heaven—we need it here on earth. Heaven has streets of gold and is filled with the glory of God. We are fully covered there. Inheritances are left to the living, not the dead. Being dead actually takes us out of the will and the inheritance that was legally ours is given to others. Those who die in Christ go on to their eternal reward.

The God dreams we have must be funded and fueled by our inheritance. Your inheritance is crucial to your life on earth.

Your faith—is your confidence in Father God. Your identity—is Father God's confidence in you! He expects you to use your inheritance. It is comprised of who He has made you and what He has for you. Treasures provided by Our Father can only be accessed by our identity as His sons—privileged, favored sons.

Place your hand over your heart and declare these words: "Because He loves me the best, I will expect the best! And I will receive the best! He is my Father! He strengthens me. His wisdom is mine at request. My Father has given me an abundant life."

He is the only father that has the ability to love every child the best—look at the cross one more time. Do you get it? He deeply loves the world! He deeply loves you!

Fatherless Parties

The prodigal was partying away his inheritance on "friends" who did not love him, while the older son was waiting for his father to throw him a party with his friends. Neither desired their father's presence at their parties—they only wanted their friends.

This is the heart of the problem with both sons—fatherless parties. There is a celebration going on in Heaven and it's around the throne of God—but it is not about the throne or the throne room. It's all about Father who is seated on the Throne! Scripture calls it worship.

Seeking parties without Father God's presence is nothing less than rebellion. If a youth does not want his parents' presence at his party, it is not godly. A party can be totally focused on someone's birthday or accomplishments with the Father's presence filling the room. It is an attitude, not the number of words directed towards Him. It is reflected in a heart of praise and love that goes beyond religious words and references that are disconnected from a living relationship.

True honor cannot be given or attained apart from Father God. Without His presence, all words of praise and honor spoken are empty vessels—devoid of the anointing oil of joy that only is found in His honor. All victories in the earth apart from God's presence are hollow, and they defraud the victor as he is left to celebrate himself.

Father God put honor and favor on Joseph through his natural father. Joseph chose to honor Father God through his difficult seasons of rejection—as well as the seasons of acceptance. Pharaoh recognized the honor on Joseph—who had just stepped out of prison—that was not present on anyone standing in his palace. Joseph celebrated Father God in the prison. Then Our Father celebrated him into the palace.

Dreamers who succeed and enjoy it, always place the Father's honor above man's honor. Many winners often feel empty after great victories for this one reason—they forgot to honor Father God who gave them the opportunity and the ability to succeed. Fatherless parties are filled with empty echoes and lifeless words.

The Father honors sons who honor Him. This is beyond the victories of earth and the celebrations of man. The Father's heart is the exclusive place in the universe where the victories that bring life and joy exclusively dwells!

People who honor themselves will never experience the Father's glory. When we come back to the Father, the real party begins. Ask the prodigal. The Father can throw a party for you that you could never plan for yourself. His celebration is all for you, but it's a display of who He is to us—Our Father.

In the party for the prodigal, the son was celebrating his great father and the father was celebrating his restored son. When you experience the party your Father throws for you—you will hear His celebration over you. Let your voice of gratitude fill His house too! It will shift your identity and anointing!

Whenever we leave Our Father, our "friends' start leaving us in a short time. Then famine starts closing in on our lives and soon thereafter we are feeding pigs. Our desire to celebrate life without the Father is an event that is guaranteed to eventually break down. He makes sure it breaks down, so it leads us back to Him.

Fatherless parties will lead prodigals to join themselves to another citizen in a foreign land—who literally does not care about them at all—because they did not care about their father at all.

Why did Cain kill Abel? Father God celebrated Abel's worship, but not Cain's. Cain's focus was not about Father God, but about his worship. It is the same attitude of Lucifer, who loved his ability to worship God—but truly desired it for himself.

Lucifer planned his own party without Father God's presence. If you drift away from your Father God, you will be greeted by "friends" who are not friends. As long as you can afford it, they will stay. They will help you destroy your inheritance, as the enemy attempts to reduce you to a slave. When the pigs surround you and the famine has crushed your carnal dreams—you will remember your Father's love.

Sinners and Sons

We must put this parable in context so that we do not miss the truth Jesus was teaching. The first two parables, the lost sheep and the lost coin, were told to the Pharisees and the teachers of the law to help them understand why He was welcoming the sinners and the tax collectors—and even eating with them! The religious leaders were upset with Jesus.

The first two stories are about *lost sinners* and the last one is about *two lost sons*. The last story was instructive to the disgruntled religious leaders standing in front of Him—as well as the rejected group who was also listening. He loved both groups and the activity of neither.

The Pharisees and the teachers of the law were coming to Jesus to challenge Him. The tax collectors and sinners were coming to hear Him.

The religious leaders were teaching people to avoid sinners so they could remain holy. Jesus was entreating them to change their hearts. They did not care about those who were lost, so they criticized Jesus to justify their lack of love.

The more time we spend with Him, the more we will be like Him. Jesus is teaching them not to be like the older son who would not come into the Father's celebration of his prodigal brother.

In the first parable, Jesus spoke of a shepherd with a hundred sheep who left the ninety-nine to search for the one that was missing. Jesus often taught in the temple, but now he was leaving the temple and looking for that "lost one."

The next parable was a woman with ten coins who did not wait until morning, but lit a lamp to search at night for the one coin that was lost. She would not wait for the light of the morning to make it easier. She was lighting her lamp and looking for that "lost one" during the inconvenient darkness.

These first two parables focus on lost sinners. In each parable they are described with this same phrase, "over one sinner who repents." Jesus used these two parables to explain to the Pharisees and the teachers of the law why He was spending time with the sinners and tax collectors. Jesus is teaching them the value of those that are lost and the immediate focus and priority they have with the Father. Every child of God should have the same values as their Father God.

The value of the lost sheep spurred the Good Shepherd to leave the ninety-nine. The value of the lost coin drove the woman into an immediate search. She also expected her friends to rejoice with her as soon as she found it—before daylight.

The third parable is not the same theme as the first two. It is dealing with lost sons, not lost sinners. It's about the struggle of two sons. Jesus is speaking of sons who do not know how to relate to their father. As you read through these parables, notice the difference.

The Parable of the Lost Sheep

Then all the tax collectors and the sinners drew near to Him to hear Him. And the Pharisees and scribes complained, saying, "This Man receives sinners and eats with them." So He spoke this parable to them, saying:

"What man of you, having a hundred sheep, if he loses one of them, does not leave the ninety-nine in the wilderness, and go after the one which is lost until he finds it? And when he has found it, he lays it on his shoulders, rejoicing. And when he comes home, he calls together his friends and neighbors, saying to them, 'Rejoice with me, for I have found my sheep which was lost!' I say to you that likewise there will be more joy in Heaven over one sinner who repents than over ninety-nine just persons who need no repentance.

Parable of the Lost Coin

"Or what woman, having ten silver coins, if she loses one coin, does not light a lamp, sweep the house, and search carefully until she finds it? ⁹ And when she has found it, she calls her friends and neighbors together, saying, 'Rejoice with me, for I have found the piece which I lost!' ¹⁰ Likewise, I say to

you, there is joy in the presence of the angels of God over one sinner who repents."

Parable of the Lost Son

Then He said: "A certain man had two sons. And the younger of them said to his father, 'Father, give me the portion of goods that falls to me.' So he divided to them his livelihood. And not many days after, the younger son gathered all together, journeyed to a far country, and there wasted his possessions with prodigal living. But when he had spent all, there arose a severe famine in that land and he began to be in want. Then he went and joined himself to a citizen of that country, and he sent him into his fields to feed swine. And he would gladly have filled his stomach with the pods that the swine ate, and no one gave him anything.

"But when he came to himself, he said, 'How many of my father's hired servants have bread enough and to spare, and I perish with hunger! I will arise and go to my father, and will say to him, "Father, I have sinned against Heaven and before you, and I am no longer worthy to be called your son. Make me like one of your hired servants." '

"And he arose and came to his father. But when he was still a great way off, his father saw him and had compassion, and ran and fell on his neck and kissed him. And the son said to him, 'Father, I have sinned against Heaven and in your sight, and am no longer worthy to be called your son.'

"But the father said to his servants, 'Bring out the best robe and put it on him, and put a ring on his hand and sandals on his feet. And bring the fatted calf here and kill it, and let us eat and be merry; for this my son was dead and is alive again; he was lost and is found.' And they began to be merry.

"Now his older son was in the field. And as he came and drew near to the house, he heard music and dancing. So he called one of the servants and asked what these things meant. And he said to him, 'Your brother has come, and because he has received him safe and sound, your father has killed the fatted calf.'

"But he was angry and would not go in. Therefore his father came out and pleaded with him. So he answered and said to his father, 'Lo, these many years I have been serving you; I never transgressed your commandment at any time; and yet you never gave me a young goat that I might make merry with my friends. But as soon as this son of yours came, who has devoured your livelihood with harlots; you killed the fatted calf for him.'

"And he said to him, 'Son, you are always with me, and all that I have is yours. It was right that we should make merry and be glad, for your brother was dead and is alive again, and was lost and is found.' "[8]

---

[8] *The New King James Version.* (1982). (Lk 15:1–32). Nashville: Thomas Nelson.

Two Sons—Two Attitudes

The main theme of the last parable is centered on the great desire Father God has to restore His sons who are separated from Him. There are many other sub-themes and insights into our Father God that should not be overlooked. This parable reveals the relationships of two sons with their father—as well as the heart of the father.

Jesus used two different sons to expose two different attitudes that exist in each of us—the selfishness and rebellion of the younger son, and the self-righteousness attitude and lack of mercy of the older son. Self-righteousness is the beautiful face of rebellion against Father God. Lack of mercy is the heart of selfishness. The two brothers were more alike than different.

The Father's sons were lost and dead with these attitudes. Sons have delayed and downsized their destiny because they refused to come to the Father and His love. He is waiting today for you to come back to the Father to be forgiven, restored and celebrated.

The older son was upset because his younger brother had received his inheritance, and he, the older son, had not. His brother had wasted the inheritance his father gave him—and now he was now being celebrated. This was not right! He was not upset how his prodigal brother had treated his father, because he was none the better. Why was he so upset?

When the father gave the prodigal his inheritance, he divided it between His two sons. All that was left with his father after the prodigal left with his inheritance belonged to the older brother. The fatted calf that was saved for special occasions—belonged to him. His father was now serving it to his prodigal brother who just returned. It was his fatted calf and the celebration that his father never gave him! He was angry.

The Father's celebrations are in His house, not in His fields. Our Father's parties are not for you and your friends—it's with Him and His family.

The fields represent His assignments—His works. The house represents His dwelling place—His presence. What we have accomplished in the fields will be celebrated in His house—in His presence.

His presence was with us in the fields; now our presence should be in His house. We cannot draw life from the fields of our accomplishments, only from His presence. There is godly satisfaction that accompanies the works of God that He has called us to do—but the celebration of those works will be held in His house, away from the fields, to keep clarity in our spirit.

The oldest son was more concerned about his inheritance, than his father or his brother. It had become the focus of his heart, blocking his ability to receive it. According to Jewish custom as the first-born male, he received a double portion so that he could replace the role of his father when he was deceased to meet the needs of any of his siblings for financial help. It would come out of the second portion that was under his care—a father's role as the first born.

His second portion was gone the moment his prodigal brother returned since there were no other siblings. He had his father's wealth, but not his heart. He was not interested in extending his father's love and mercy to his prodigal brother who had wasted his inheritance—who now qualified for his financial care. How would you feel if you were the oldest son? Are you a son with the father's heart?

Our relationship with Father God will ultimately determine if we will mishandle our inheritance, totally miss it or live from it. All of us will experience each dimension in different seasons and assignments, but our goal is to live out of our inheritance. To miss our inheritance may be as great of a sin as wasting it. Idolizing it is the worst.

Rejoice With Me

In each parable, every person searching for what was lost wanted all to rejoice with them as soon as it was found. Everyone did—except the oldest brother in the last parable.

Our Father God set parameters for His restorations. There is no restoration without revelation repentance. If the prodigal said he was sorry for what he had done, it would only be an assessment of his bad behavior. His focus would still be on himself.

The prodigal had a revelation of the relationship he had broken with his father—focusing on his father. This is the key to true repentance—we see our Father's love greater than our own sins. Our heart is filled with Him, not ourselves. We are centered on His goodness, not our badness.

The parable ends with the father going out to the missing elder son who would not join his father's celebration in his house. The eldest son was standing outside the house—in his father's fields. He was still a lost son.

As soon as the restoration is declared by Our Father, He expects all of his sons to leave the fields to rejoice with Him—in His house. The older son would not enter and rejoice. He stood in the field of his good works—angry at his father's mercy towards his brother.

When we rejoice with our Father God over our restored brothers—it infuses us with His heart and strength for our future battles. If we will not rejoice with our Father, His strength will leave us and we will fail.

He will not allow our goodness to be our strength. Our integrity will become an idol if we do not perceive that it flows from Him. Mercy in our heart is the root of holiness for life—it's the heart of Our Father. Mercy is the gate to the throne room of holiness—not an excuse to live at the edge of hell. Our Father God is the strength of our heart; He is our integrity.

Whom have I in heaven but You? And there is none upon earth that I desire besides You. My flesh and my heart fail; But God is the strength of my heart and my portion forever.[9]

Inheritance Laws

Then came the daughters of Zelophehad the son of Hepher, the son of Gilead, the son of Machir, the son of Manasseh, from the families of Manasseh the son of Joseph; *and these*

---

[9] *The New King James Version.* (1982). (Ps 73:25–26). Nashville: Thomas Nelson.

were the names of his daughters: Mahlah, Noah, Hoglah, Milcah, and Tirzah. And they stood before Moses, before Eleazar the priest, and before the leaders and all the congregation, by the doorway of the tabernacle of meeting, saying: "Our father died in the wilderness; but he was not in the company of those who gathered together against the LORD, *in company with Korah, but he died in his own sin; and he had no sons. Why should the name of our father be removed from among his family because he had no son? Give us a possession among our father's brothers."*

So Moses brought their case before the LORD. *And the* LORD *spoke to Moses, saying: "The daughters of Zelophehad speak what is right; you shall surely give them a possession of inheritance among their father's brothers, and cause the inheritance of their father to pass to them.* [10]

This is an amazing story with two noteworthy conversations: the daughters spoke to Moses; then God spoke to Moses. Father God loved their request and recorded it in scripture to set a precedent.

If these five sisters had not asked for their inheritance based on who they were to God and Israel, Moses would not have agreed to hear them—let alone consider their request. They stood as daughters of Joseph, rather than daughters with no inheritance. Our identity is the key to access our

---

[10] *The New King James Version.* (1982). (Nu 27:1–7). Nashville: Thomas Nelson.

inheritance. We may have millions of dollars in our bank account, but we cannot access a penny without our identity.

After establishing our identity, we must ask in the presence of Our Father—even though we may be talking to another person. We should believe that Father God will affect that person's decision because we are factoring in Our Father's favor and influence.

They were standing by the doorway of the Tabernacle. Their request was made in the presence of God before Moses. They were comfortable and respectful in that gate of authority. They were not angry at God or those in authority for the loss they had experienced, but they did expect a shift in their situation. Do you? They asked for their inheritance with faith that they would receive it.

If we have judgments against the essence of authority or people in authority—we will never be able to utilize it to reach our destiny or to help others. Heaven is filled with authority—Hell has none. Do not confuse oppression, abuse, or rebellion with authority. Just as man's sin and selfishness corrupted a perfect garden, those qualities have also corrupted authority.

They stood before Moses in the shadow of Joseph. They stood before justice in the light of favor. Stand before your Father God in the glory of Jesus when you ask for your inheritance. The favor of Joseph is multiplied in Jesus.

These daughters were the descendants of Joseph—the one who ruled in Egypt. They believed God's favor was still on their family because of him. Their ancestry list stopped at Joseph for a reason. They knew who had the favor in their family line before Father God and Israel.

Leverage your inheritance requests before Father God— mention your family connection to Jesus! Stop at Jesus. Connect yourself to the favor of The Father because of The Son.

Learn to clearly present your case in the gates of Heaven before your "Moses" in the presence of the Father—and your lost inheritance will be restored! We must be comfortable presenting our cases before men on the earth for God to shift it from Heaven. It is a fact that fifty-one percent of working people could have a pay raise but they will not ask for it. Asking is a powerfully vulnerable business for the secure.

Asking—The Privilege of Sons.

Then He said: "A certain man had two sons. And the younger of them said to his father, 'Father, give me the portion of goods that falls to me.' So he divided to them his livelihood." (Luke 15:11,12 NKJV)

Asking is not as easy as it first appears. It is much more than saying what you want, but that is also included. Some have a difficulty *asking* what they desire. They have lost their voice of authority and granted favor. Others have a difficulty *knowing* what they desire. They have lost hope, which feeds faith that produces vision for destiny. What we see determines our future.

The younger son did not have an intimate relationship with his father, but he knew what his father had belonged to him. He recognized how to receive it—just ask. We often write off the prodigal son as simply rebellious. Yet, he had revelation of his father in the midst of his selfishness that his older brother did not have in the midst of his goodness.

Asking is the privilege of sons—an authority hidden from orphans. Orphans beg—sons ask. Sons live in the revelation that Father God gives an inheritance upon request. God so loved the world that He gave. Father God is a giver—mankind is an earner.

Heaven will not function within earth's fallen rules projected by Satan and enforced by our natural reasoning. It is not about what we deserve. The key issue is "What can we receive as sons?"

Even though Our Father gave His Son, He must be received—and that is impossible without revelation. Likewise, revelation is required to receive our inheritance—I am His son! It's more than words repeated—it's a revelation.

A son has unspoken privileges in his father's house that the employer of his father will never enjoy. A son can open his father's refrigerator, looking for what he desires. His father's employer may be the wealthiest man in town, but he does not have refrigerator rights in his employee's house.

Even if that employer owned the house and the refrigerator his employee rented, he could inspect the refrigerator, but he cannot live out of it—he is still not a son!

What we are doing with what we already have is a qualifier to stepping into a greater portion of our inheritance. It is also based on our obedient response to the request of Our Father. Our willingness reveals our active sonship.

Remember, our access to our inheritance is multi-dimensional. Our bank account can be accessed by check, scams, credit card, robbers, driver's licenses, hacks, contracts, electronic transfers, embezzlements, automatic payments, and other numerous methods. Keep an eye on your inheritance— the enemy is, and so is your Father! The enemy does not have the ability to rob it from Our Father, but he knows how to run a scam on us. Don't be fooled.

Are we ready to utilize our kingdom inheritance? It is released to those with kingdom plans. Until your God dream has plans, it is not yet a vision. Provision is given to planned vision.

Opportunities to receive from Heaven are most often granted by Father God at the request of His sons. Father God may start the conversation as He comes to us, but we, as sons, must still request what we need. Think of Moses's questions at the burning bush: "Whom shall I say sent me? What if they don't believe me?"

Moses received what he needed upon request. We often miss the obvious. Father God gave Moses the burning bush.

Moses requested God's name. He also received a miracle rod of authority because he asked, "How will the people know that You have sent me?" Moses would need both to accomplish his mission.

When a son asks of his father, it should be obtained based on the father's goodness, not the son's. Yet the Father's goodness resident in that son will often determine the long-term fruitfulness of what he obtains.

Our faith can obtain an inheritance that our present maturity cannot maintain. Ask the prodigal. Not every portion received is a certification of our maturity. Some inheritance portions are given are a tremendous opportunity given by The Father inviting us to the next level with instructions to help us grow.

Our Father is strategically trying to build our foundation in Him, not in our accomplishments. It is required by Our Father as He searches throughout the earth to find those through whom He can show Himself strong.

Our prayer life is often where we make our requests known to Father God. Yet, our prayer list is often our problem list. We need to move from our problem prayer list to our seed dream list—and what we need to accomplish it. It is instinctive to pray for existing problems. It is unnatural to pray consistently, strategically, and purposefully over our dreams—but it is very necessary. Our prayer life sets vision in our thoughts and dreams in our hearts—giving us the ability to creatively enter our destiny.

We can actually pray and never ask The Father for anything. We may talk to Him about the problem, but never ask Him what we actually need.

As I started studying the issue of inheritances, I realized the importance and the blessing of an inheritance. Out of the desire of my heart I cried out to the Lord; "My father did not give me an inheritance, but I am asking you Father God for my inheritance. I want my inheritance. I am asking for my inheritance." I kept asking Father God for my inheritance.

After a year had passed, a man walked up to me that I had never met before. He was close to my father's age. He said, "I want to help your ministry. I have some stock I want to give you. It could become very valuable someday." The value of the stock has not reached its day, but what grabbed my attention was his last name—Mast. It marked the beginning my inheritance season.

The heavens opened over my life in so many ways and my Father God started giving me my inheritance. It has continued to this day. I wrote my first book, *And David Perceived He Was King*. I would like to share with you an excerpt from it.

The crown was set on his head, but it still wasn't established in his thoughts, his vision, or his actions. David had reached God's goal and his destiny, but he had not yet perceived that the Lord had established him as king over Israel. Father God sent King Hiram to help David settle this issue.

King Hiram of Tyre sent an envoy to David . . . to build him a royal palace. (1 Chron. 14:1 MSG)

There comes a time in every David's life when God uses another king to build us a "White House." This shifts our identity into our purpose and activities. It will bring a greater honor, releasing a greater anointing in our life (pg. 223).

Father God supernaturally caused our house to be sold when we had taken it off of the market for over a year. He directed us to buy a house in another county north of our previous address. As we were leaving our new house, I heard Father God ask me a question: "Where do you live?" I didn't think about our street address as He led my mind to the name of the county—*New Castle.*

It was built by a developer as his house. It has more features than I would have ever pursued for myself. I love the five acres of peaceful land and the swimming pool. My Father God did for me what He did for David—when I asked for my inheritance. For my wife, it was restoration and beyond what she asked. You are a privileged son in the eyes of your Father—ask.

Heart Relationship—The Key to Your Requests

Then Caleb said, "Whoever attacks Kirjath Sepher and takes it, to him I will give my daughter Achsah as wife." And Othniel the son of Kenaz, Caleb's younger brother, took it; so he gave him his daughter Achsah as wife. Othniel took it, so Caleb gave him his daughter Acsah as his wife. When she arrived she got him to ask for farmland from her father.

As she dismounted from her donkey Caleb asked her, "What would you like?" She said, "Give me a marriage gift. You've given me desert land; now, give me pools of water!" And he gave her the upper and the lower pools.[11]

Caleb was a man of faith and a fierce warrior who cried, "Give me my mountain!" As a young man, he still believed they could take the Promised Land after seeing the giants. The fear that gripped Israel did not sway his faith. He still believed — so God preserved his life to lead the next generation into that victory.

As an older father, he was looking for a husband for his daughter who could protect her in the newly acquired land he had just taken from giants. Caleb knew other tribes and nations that would test Israel's resolve to keep that which God had given them.

Caleb put out an invitational challenge among the warriors with an unusual reward. "Whoever attacks this city and takes it, to him I will give my daughter." The first one to attack the city would be a decisive fearless leader. Othniel was the warrior who had the spirit to win the challenge — and he did!

Caleb was bringing his daughter to Othniel for marriage. Achsah, the daughter of Caleb, wanted more than a husband — she wanted her inheritance. She knew the window of opportunity that was in front of Othniel, but he did not perceive it.

---

[11] Peterson, E. H. (2005). *The Message: the Bible in contemporary language* (Jdg 1:11–15). Colorado Springs, CO: NavPress.

Warriors that have the ability to take cities—often have difficulty receiving. Many battles in life are required to succeed against the enemy. A battle-ready mentality can block our ability to ask at strategic times. We must hold the hand of Our Father as we cling to the Sword of the Spirit. He was Our Father first.

She had the timing, and she urged her champion to ask for a field. She knew her father was moved by victories and faith. Othniel requested the farmland, but it was actually desert land that her father gave him.

Achsah, Caleb's daughter, got off her donkey to come before her father to receive what she wanted. Even though Othniel had asked for the fields, she restated it to her father, "You've given me desert land; now give me pools of water!"

When Othniel asked for the field, Caleb replied "yes"— but his eyes were fixed on his daughter, not the warrior. Caleb may have seen her urging him to ask. Achsah knew at that point she had more favor in the eyes of her father as a daughter, than he, the warrior who had taken the city. Othniel, the victorious warrior, quietly stood still as he realized his bride had unlimited favor with her father, Caleb.

Never forget this principle as you approach your Father— bring out your sonship, not your victories.

She did not urge her fiancé to make another request, but she went in front of her father and leveraged her relationship with him to get exactly what she wanted. Caleb asked his daughter, "What would you like?" as she was walking toward her father.

Many of us believe that Our Father will not give us what we desire. We confuse our training and maturing season by Our Father—with His heart for our personal desires. Notice in this story, the father asked her that question before she made her request known. The father's desire to bless his daughter was in his heart—and it's already in the heart of Our Father for each of us.

You must get off your donkey and ask. Don't talk to your father from his provision, talk to him from your heart. The daughter left what her father had provided for her journey *as a bride* and walked towards him *as his daughter.*

Our walk towards Our Father should display a confident expectation that causes Him to ask, "What do you want?" Our approach to Him speaks of our relationship and belief concerning Him in our lives. Work on your walk to your Father as a son. Get closer—don't talk from a distance. You are a son—not a stranger. Get closer than you have ever been before.

There are many titles that people put before my name as I have pastored over three decades and traveled to the nations. Before I speak in a new place, I will often—if not always, kneel before my Father and pray.

"Father, this is your son, Dale. I am asking you to help me touch these people so they would know what an awesome Father you are. Thank You, Father, for the authority and anointing you give me as your son to strengthen the people, this church and to shift this nation towards you. Surprise me with your presence and wisdom as I teach and minister. Let the people be in awe of You and closer to You when I am done. You created me to do this. Thank you Father for helping this son."

I sense His pleasure—I am aware of His presence—I see His power—I hear His voice—I know His heart—He is My Father. He is your Father! Step into Him. You are His son. You are His daughter.

There are other things I say as well, depending where I am at that time, but I do not come to Him with any other titles—just *son*. Son trumps every other title of importance. Who you are to Him is greater than who He makes you to people. Keep it simple—it's about all any of us can handle.

Desert farmland without water rights was undesirable. Othniel may have taken a city, but the daughter had taken her father's heart. Othniel received the desert lands, but only the daughter could request the streams and pools of water— the most valuable asset.

What Caleb did not give to a victorious warrior, he would give upon request to the daughter he loved. She sensed her privileged position in her father's eyes—and she accessed it. She asked for the pools of water and her father gave her the upper and lower pools of water—more than she expected.

It is also interesting to note that Caleb's daughter was knowledgeable of the land that her father had conquered. She was looking it over—thinking of her inheritance.

Do you know what your Father God has conquered? Do you believe you have an inheritance? Do you understand that what He has conquered is available to you upon your request as a son or daughter? You will not obtain it just because you are a victorious warrior or even His son—you will obtain it at your request as you move closer to Him.

If you feel there is something missing in your life, you may just have to get off your donkey and ask for what you want—or you may end up living a very dry life, filled with difficulties because you have refused to come before Father God with great expectations. Ask for the rivers.

He is a good, good Father. We have made Him God, and He is—but know Him as a good, good Father—Our Father.

Carnal Promises

I was going through one of the most difficult times in my life as my son's birthday was approaching. We decided to get a Golden Retriever for our youngest son. Every place I called the entire litter was already been sold, even though the young pups still needed to be with their mother. I was informed by one breeder that I needed to plan at least a year ahead to secure a good puppy. I called the last ad in desperation, only to find it was totally sold as well. One puppy had been reserved, but the buyer had not paid for it, nor set a time to pick it up. The buyer said that the first one to come with the money would have the puppy.

During the forty-five minute drive in the rain that seemed like two hours, I cried out to God. I felt very alone on a dreary day, in the midst of several major unresolved battles. "God, I am down to believing you for a dog. I need to know that you still see me and hear me." As the sun broke through the rain, a vibrant double rainbow appeared like none other I had ever seen. Within an hour I was driving home with the puppy in a box, thanking my Father God for hearing my smallest prayer in the midst of great turmoil.

It gave me strength to navigate into my new season. Why? I knew He heard me and He met me in a very personal way. I did not try to obtain what I desired by promising God that I would give Him more.

In the Bible, people sometimes promised personal sacrifices to God before entering the battle for victory—as if man's chosen sacrifices motivated God to help. If our carnal promises intersect at His divine purposes, we are simply agreeing with Him in a highly dysfunctional way. We can receive many things from Father God without a correct relationship with Him—as the prodigal demonstrated.

Many times God helps us in spite of what we have promised, not because of it. The only sacrifices that God accepts are the ones that He chooses. Self-sacrifice is a religious spirit trying to gain God's favor, while believing we are still rejected by Him.

Jephthah made a vow to the Lord and said, "If You will indeed give the sons of Ammon into my hand, then it shall be that whatever comes out of the doors of my house to meet me when I return in peace from the sons of Ammon, it shall be the Lord's, and I will offer it up as a burnt offering." [12]

Jephthah was a gifted warrior that was driven away from his homeland by his half-brothers, as he was a child of a

---

[12] *New American Standard Bible: 1995 update.* (1995). (Jdg 11:30–31). LaHabra, CA: The Lockman Foundation.

prostitute. They did not want him to have a share in the family inheritance. Upon facing the enemy, the elders of the town brought him back and agreed to make him the ruler—if he was victorious over the Ammonites. The scripture records that the Spirit of God came upon Jephthah. It was all he needed, as Father God had already promised victory over the enemy to His people when they looked to Him.

Jephthah lived as an orphan, not a son with an inheritance. The elders of the town—not his brothers—brought him back with promised rewards based on his expected victory. The rejection of this world is real and it was in force against him. Jephthah projected that same pattern towards God. He promised God a reward for his victory—the first thing that came out the door of his house when he returned home—he would offer as a burnt sacrifice. His request for victory over the enemy was based on a sacrifice he had chosen, rather than what Father God had promised.

He had no basis to believe that Father God would give him a victory. He did not feel valued by his natural father who did nothing as his half-brothers drove him away. Therefore he could not believe that Father God valued him enough to help him. The enemy will always use "brothers," or circumstances to devalue our identity as a son. The enemy will also use what our father did not do for us—to destroy healthy expectations of our Father God. As worthless fellows went with him, they simply reinforced his lack of value. He had allowed these hurts to shape his heart and his relationship to Father God.

Jephthah believed that he had no value to Father God personally, so he decided he would give Him something of value. Do you understand his reasoning? Asking is often based on perceived personal value in the eyes of the giver. If there is no perceived value in the person asking, *they must create it.*

Jephthah needed to enter the battle as a loved son standing in his Father's promises, not his. Father God created Jephthah a mighty warrior to win victories for Him and Israel. Jephthah did not equate his gift as a warrior as part of his inheritance as a son. It was the Father's strength and fearless boldness in him that made him a warrior. The spirit of insignificance fuels pride. If we cannot overcome it, we must create value based on personal performance or personal promises. It is the heart of religion; a belief system based in man's goodness. It produces a critical attitude. It has the same effect as standing in quicksand—the more we do, the deeper we sink.

Unrepentant fear and guarded pride could not embrace the change that Jesus was offering to the hearts of some men of prominence. Their insecurity forced them to bring an end to the messenger from The Father—His Son, Jesus. Our insecurity will force us to kill the dreams we are carrying and desiring. We must receive the redemptive changes that Father God scheduled in our journey on earth to bring us into the fullness of His life in us. Only in His love can we realize the value we have in His eyes.

After the great victory, Jephthah returned home only to be greeted by his daughter coming out the door. In those days, animals were often kept inside of houses at night to keep them from being stolen. Since closing doors were not always used, it would be common to have animals walking in and out of the house doorway during the day. God's word forbade the sacrificing of children.

This story clearly illustrates that God does not need, or want our useless religious sacrifices we chose to gain authority. He chose the ultimate sacrifice, Jesus. If there is anything He desires for you to sacrifice in your life, He will let you know.

The religious spirit begs as an orphan, or demands compensation as a striving employee. The orphan spirit entered the world through the fall of Adam and Eve. Father God was coming to be with them and they were hiding in shame, trying to cover their nakedness by the work of their hands.

Father God is coming to be with us. When will we learn to lean into who He is and who we are to Him? Our purpose and His will intersect as we come out of hiding. "Where are you?" is the question of the ages. The Father was not trying to gain information. He was helping them realize where they had chosen to live—in hiding. His heart did not abandon them. He was still coming for them after they sinned.

The Importance of Your Inheritance

When a will is read, each child is inwardly holding their breath, as they are receiving from their parents for the last time. It can be about the money or significant items, but it really is about the love and the value added to each child who receives from the parents through the will.

The monetary value of an inheritance is often determined by the level of relationship to that person. While friends may receive several items, sons and daughters always receive the lion's share of an inheritance, if not all of it—unless there was a broken relationship.

There is a realm of healing and affirmation in receiving an inheritance. Whatever is given is the last celebration by their parents and the last validation by them—as their loved child.

The inheritance from Our Father is an indicator of the type of relationship we enjoy with Him—sons! Everything Our Father gives us speaks of who He is to us and who we are to Him. We can study the truths of the scriptures focusing on how it works—and start to forget who is working it— Our Father!

Inheritances are set by Our Father God and activated by the depth of our relationship to the Him. Sons are the determiners of the depth of that relationship—as Jesus has opened the door wide to all of us.

Anger and judgments against Father God are huge blocks to receiving a godly inheritance. Ask Father God to reveal any anger or judgments residing in you that are actually against Him. The enemy will try to hide it from our eyes to block our ability to move forward into our destiny with Father God.

What has you angry in life? More often than not, a judgment against God is hidden in that anger. Anger steals the anointing and releases counterfeit wisdom that moves us from the will of Our Father.

The God of peace will soon crush Satan underneath our feet. Ungodly anger will ruin our destiny and our ability to crush him. It is the enemy's attempt to weaken our relationship with our Father, the source of our authority and vision.

Connecting To Our Father

And in that day you will ask Me nothing. Most assuredly, I say to you, whatever you ask the Father in My name He will give you. Until now you have asked nothing in My name. Ask, and you will receive, that your joy may be full. (John 16:23–24 NKJV)

Jesus was revealing to his disciples about the mega-shift coming soon. Whenever they had a need, they asked Jesus for help. Jesus was about to leave earth. He was preparing them how to ask when He was gone. They were not to pray to Him, but to the Father.

Jesus came to connect us to Abba Father. We are now in the day when we ask the Father, in the name of Jesus. We are accessing Heaven with His identity.

Our joy is full when we receive from Father God, because it reveals our relationship to Him and His direct love for us. There was no joy in the prodigal son when he received his inheritance. He did not value or perceive his father's love for him—his focus was on his inheritance.

We can still ask Jesus to help us, but our eyes must be opened to the fact that Jesus is giving us access to the Father. The joy of answered prayer is that He hears us and He loves us! He knows us and the situations that we are facing. He is for us and with us!

Father God is always doing more for us than we expected. Did He really need to shake the place after they were finished praying in Acts 4:31 as they were facing persecution? They didn't ask for it. Father God will rock your world to let you know He loves you and He is with you! His is Our Father who watches over us.

Jesus said to him, "I am the way, the truth, and the life. No one comes to the Father except through Me.[13]

Jesus is not the way to Heaven, but the way to the Father. Heaven is included—it's our Father's address!

The debilitating orphan spirit attempts to drive us to prove our value. Striving always ends in bitter disappointments and the enemy knows it. God will not enter into a relationship based on what we do, but rather according to our response to what He has done or spoken.

---

[13] *The New King James Version*. (1982). (Jn 14:6). Nashville: Thomas Nelson.

Jesus was not only the way to The Father, but He was also is the exact and perfect expression of Our Father. If we see Jesus for who He is—we know the Father as well. We are called as His sons and daughters to introduce and demonstrate Father God to lost sinners and lost sons.

His Hallowed Name — Our Father

For you did not receive the spirit of bondage again to fear, but you received the Spirit of adoption by whom we cry out, "Abba, Father." The Spirit Himself bears witness with our spirit that we are children of God, and if children, then heirs — heirs of God and joint heirs with Christ, if indeed we suffer with Him, that we may also be glorified together.[14]

There is a fear of rejection that tries to keep believers identified as sinners saved by grace. It can actually be a huge barrier to our destiny and the relationship Father God now desires versus the correct assessment of our salvation. Our identity must shift from sinners saved by grace to sons of The Father.

Entering The Father's celebration accelerates our destiny in immeasurable ways that are easily observed by others. Even this world is tired of orphans that celebrate themselves. It is unfitting for the sons of the Father to do the same, but if you do not enter into His celebration you are forced by design to create your own — attempting to avoid depression and lack of value.

Just as Our Father created a celebration around Himself, you were made in His image and likeness — created to be celebrated. We are celebrated; He is celebrated and worshiped. All the angels rejoice when one soul is saved. But he has

---

[14] *The New King James Version.* (1982). (Ro 8:15–17). Nashville: Thomas Nelson.

restrained everything in Heaven from celebrating your life in Him—He has reserved that for Himself—that's Our Father!

His Holy Spirit cries through us, "Abba, Father!" to connect us to Him. It is not natural for the spirit of man to cry out to God as Father. We need to allow His Spirit to shift our spirit into the new creation relationship with Father God as a son. This requires more than reading these scriptures and believing them—but we must start there. He is calling us into a living relationship. We start with our mind—but we must live it from our hearts.

It is important to start calling Him Father God even if there are still orphan areas remaining in our lives. The journey towards Our Father God will shatter one area after another from our mind, spirit and identity. We can live as a son in one arena—and an orphan in another. The more you grow as a son, the more you will become aware where the enemy has beguiled you.

My daughter, Heidi, approached me after I had preached a sermon referencing Jesus teaching us to pray—"Our Father, who art in Heaven, hallowed be Thy name." She said, "Dad, that must mean that the hallowed name of God is Our Father." It was very special coming from my daughter. All of us know this prayer—but were we listening? His hallowed name we just spoke is *Our Father.*

If my children call me *Dale* it is actually disrespectful of my position in their life. *Mr. Mast* is unacceptable as well. There is only one name I will accept from them—Dad

(Father). When we speak to Father God, we often are addressing him as "Mr. God." I do not think it is respectful to His position in our lives.

I stood a man and his son in the front of my church. I explained how important my role was to my church and even to the nations. Even so, this young boy will receive from his father things that are not available to me. Being a son trumps being important. If someone were picking on this young boy, I would be there to intervene as a good pastor, but his father would be there two steps before me. He is the father—the young boy is *his son*.

How much more is your Father God watching over you and what is happening around you? There is an increased protection that flows from a father to a son. Father God does not just want to be your God—He wants to be your Father. This is an incredible privileged position He desires in your life. Remember, He "rebirthed" you to life—if you are born again. He is your Father. You have son privileges with Father God.

For as many as are led by the Spirit of God, these are sons of God. [15]

As we are led by the Spirit of Father God, He will position our relationship to Father God as sons. The Spirit of Father God will help us to think like sons. The Holy Spirit cries through us to Father God—Abba Father! His voice

[15] *The New King James Version*. (1982). (Ro 8:14). Nashville: Thomas Nelson.

dismantles the orphan spirit of this world that the enemy has spoken over us.

One of the purposes of the Holy Spirit is to keep us in that identity. Even as He helps us worship Father God, He is positioning us as sons before Father God. Being led by the Spirit of God—is simply living in Our Father!

The Holy Spirit is crying through us "Abba, Father!" He will always lead us into The Father's presence. Each time we speak that hallowed name, Father—we are reminded that we are sons of favor and privilege.

If we call Him Father and refuse to be led by the Spirit of God, we are not living as sons to Him. He is making our hearts sensitive to His leading so we do not miss Him or our destiny.

A Warning against Worldliness

*W*here do wars and fights come from among you? Do they not come from your desires for pleasure that war in your members? You lust and do not have. You murder and covet and cannot obtain. You fight and war. Yet you do not have because you do not ask. You ask and do not receive, because you ask amiss, that you may spend it on your pleasures. [16]

In this warning against worldliness, we see the obvious attitudes of very carnal Christians. Murder, fighting and quarreling are listed before James speaks of the sin of not asking. Part of worldliness among Christians is that they will not ask God for what they want. Lack of asking is a sign of a lack of relationship! The refusal to ask God for what we need is listed as the first reason that we don't have what we need. Then James lists the second reason—we are asking God selfishly. That is amazing!

---

[16] *The New King James Version*. (1982). (Jas 4:1–3). Nashville: Thomas Nelson.

Asking is truly a difficult task for many of us. We prefer to do good deeds, hoping to qualify for a blessing rather than to simply ask for our Father's help. Godly asking is based on intimate friendship and innocent trust.

The orphan spirit deceives us into believing that we are unwanted, ignored, and unloved by the father. The orphan spirit manipulates our mind to believe that we will be recognized and loved by our stellar, award-winning performance. The deception increases the confusion. Are we loved for who we are, or for what we do?

The prodigal son knew something about his father that the older, more mature brother did not know—*asking with expectation as a son is the key to receiving from the father.*

Even though his relationship with his father and his maturity was sadly lacking, he had keen insight into his father. He was not yet acquainted with his father's heart—nor was he interested, but he understood how to receive his inheritance. He simply asked as a son. A son knows his father's favor will perform his requests.

Growing up as children, it did not take us long to figure out who to ask for what. There were certain things we could get from our Dad and other things we could get from our Mom. Grandparents were more likely to give us gifts on visits, but parents did better on our birthdays and Christmas. Certain friends would give us what our parents didn't want us to have.

We learned how to get what we wanted from different relationships. There are principles in this system as we face life that can be helpful, but it also creates problems. We now know how to get what we want when it is not His will, way or timing. We also have sources apart from Our Father and His direction.

Asking can be a very vulnerable position for any of us. Refusal can be devastating if trust is not at the center of our relationship with Father God. Immature children would rather take something, or earn it, than to be put in a position of possible disappointment. The orphan spirit of this world does not like to ask in faith. Begging or manipulation is the way of the world and is very different in nature than "making your requests known unto God."

Father God designed our requests to be based from a relationship with Him and understanding of His ways and thoughts. Asking should not be based in selfishness—yet it should include our desires. This makes it difficult for us to approach God with confidence in certain areas of our lives because we have not yet sorted these conflicting aspects within us.

A godly desire can become a selfish goal. A selfish goal for someone else can be a godly desire for you. It is not about the desire—*it's about you with it.*

A sign of worldliness in the church is our inability to ask Our Father. Break it and break through!

Leaving Home

*And not many days after, the younger son gath-
ered all together, journeyed to a far country,
and there wasted his possessions with prodigal living.* (Luke 15:13 NKJV)

The younger son was living with his father, but wanted
to be somewhere far away. There was no honor or desire for
his father in his heart. When the father gave his younger son
his portion, it was just days before he left.

Even though the father knew the rebellion in his son's
heart, he still granted his request. The Father does not give
to us things based on His judgment of us, but rather on how
we ask and who we are to Him. The prodigal wasted the stuff
of his inheritance while he lived a life apart from his father.
His greatest inheritance was still back at home—his father.
He had only left with his possessions.

Many believers will distant themselves from The Father
as soon as they receive the possessions of their inheritance.
We can fall into the pattern of the prodigal, without his rebellion or sinful lifestyle. We can also respond with the older
brother syndrome, judging our Father and blocking our
ability to receive the portion he set aside for us.

The prodigal correctly approached his father for his inheritance, but he did not value his father, so he could not value
what he received. Because the father valued his son, he gave

him what the son valued. It was an invitation for the prodigal son to see his heart for him.

Jesus is giving us a bird's-eye view of how Father God does business with His sons and daughters.

The inheritance was to be given upon death of the father. As Jesus told the story, those listening understood the disrespect the prodigal was showing to his father. Many were probably surprised that the father gave the inheritance to his son, upon his request, in this parable. That would not have happened in their culture.

There are times that God will honor our requests to seed into our future relationship with Him. The father honored the son's decision, knowing he would leave and waste it all. The father knew his son would have to waste what he valued so that he could see how he wasted who was valuable—his father.

The prodigal left home, but the father never left him—he was simply waiting for his return. The inheritance he had just given to his son was not precious in his eyes—his son was. The prodigal is teaching us that our inheritance is more than the possessions; it is our Father and the provision for the vision.

The Famine Season

But when he had spent all, there arose a severe
famine in that land and he began to be in want.
(Luke 15:14 NKJV)

"The Lord is my shepherd, I shall not want." If we do not allow the Lord to direct our lives, we will never be fulfilled. Want will always be a part of our life, even though we are saved. We can have Jesus as our savior, but not allow him to be our shepherd.

The prodigal experienced *want* before he received his portion. He thought it would fill the void that was in him. He spent all he had trying to fill the void. He thought about his father and his house. The pride he had, and the shame he felt, kept him from returning. The father was waiting then, but the son had not yet come to himself. The prodigal missed his first opportunity to return to his father.

The famine was the second invitation for the son to see the value of the father. The older son was still working faithfully in his father's fields, and his hidden anger was growing towards his father. He saw his father waiting and looking for the return of his younger brother. The father was not unaware of his eldest son's attitude.

In the famine season, our focus is survival. Our life view is radically redefined. Life becomes the goal. Removing the resources of his previous life helped the prodigal to identify his father as the source of true life and the key to his inheritance.

Clarity can be obtained in disastrous losses as the superficiality of success is removed, if bitterness is avoided. Transparency of truth can also be achieved from an intimate relationship with Father God in the midst of tremendous success if we love Him more than our victories. Those who know their God shall do mighty exploits. Know Him more than your victories and exploits.

It was easier for the prodigal to see his sin against his father than the older son. The prodigal wasted his inheritance while his older brother was still enamored with it. The older brother saw his father as the problem. The prodigal knew he was the problem.

The prodigal finally came to himself when he desired the food he was giving to the pigs and returned to his father. The eldest son never came to himself, nor did he return from the work of his hands to the arms of his loving father. This is very sad.

Joining

Then he went and joined himself to a citizen of that country, and he sent him into his fields to feed swine. And he would gladly have filled his stomach with the pods that the swine ate, and no one gave him anything. (Luke 15:15, 16 NKJV)

People love to join, because they believe it will make them belong. If we belong, then we are accepted. The underlying motivation for joining can be a subtle spirit of rejection. There are positive reasons for joining—it creates a greater force through unity, but joining will not remove rejection.

The seeds of rejection will follow us until we allow Our Father God to crush it with a revelation of His love for us. He crushes rejection as we draw closer to Him as our Father. It came into the earth when Adam and Eve retreated from His presence—so we must now pursue Him in response to His pursuit of us to break it. If we stop living in His presence, the spirit of rejection will return.

Family is the only place where sons belong. Father God sets us in natural families and the enemy tries to destroy them. It is the strategy of hell to block our ability to be in the family of God on this earth.

With his inheritance totally gone and now living in the midst of a famine, he dug his heels in even deeper refusing to go to his father. He joined himself to a citizen in the place he had chosen to live—a foreign land.

If we disconnect from our Father God, we will attach ourselves to a substitute father who will not meet our needs. A foreign land will never accept a *lost son*, but a *favored son* can rule in a foreign land like Joseph.

Jesus said that He was going to the Father to create a dwelling place for us. That speaks of a place in Heaven as well as a spiritual dwelling place for us to live in on earth. Before Jesus was crucified and resurrected—His disciples followed Him. After the day of Pentecost, He dwelt in them and they dwelt in Him. That is an amazing difference!

This citizen, to whom the prodigal had joined himself, did not accept him—but used him. A citizen, by definition, can never be a father. Citizen speaks of earthly nations, father speaks of family. The citizen treated him worse than the pigs he owned, refusing to feed him. We will starve if we do not live in Our Father's presence.

This citizen valued his pigs above the prodigal who was working for him—just as the prodigal valued his inheritance above his own father. The son's hard heart was breaking as he fed the pigs in the midst of the famine. The selfishness and independence that drove him from his father, now had him trapped at a pig trough—a prophetic picture of unending selfishness.

If an Israelite touched a pig, he was considered unclean. This prodigal is now being asked to care for that which he was commanded to avoid his entire life. It would be regarded as an unfit place for any Jew. The Egyptians despised the Israelites because they were shepherds. But the Jews despised tending pigs, because they were forbidden to eat them. This was a cultural value from a spiritual requirement. He was trapped into caring for and feeding what he could never enjoy in a meal.

All of the prodigal's friends treated him as he had treated his father. They only wanted what he had—not him. When they took what he had, they left him—the same way he treated his father. As the prodigal devalued the relationship with his father, so did all of his "friends."

The level of honor we give our father and mother in every aspect creates our future, forming and affecting every relationship. It empowers or limits every endeavor in our lives—even if they are not alive. We can change the level of honor we give to our parents at any time in our life.

Honor is not agreement, nor approval. It is an attitude required by Father God of all children that carries a special blessing and a promise of long life. It is a core heart issue—and Our Father knows it.

The Mirror

The prodigal is now fathering the pigs. This would be a place of revelation from his father's perspective. God was giving the prodigal "father lessons." Pigs are greedy, self-centered animals. They take what they want and leave. God was putting a large mirror in front of this selfish son—with him being the "father" and the pigs being his "sons."

As his father had taken care of him, now he was taking care of pigs on a daily basis. The prodigal was not appreciated or honored by the pigs that could not take care of themselves—the same way he never appreciated or honored his father. They came when he had something and left when it was gone—everyday! The pigs would have died without his care for them, but they did not care about him.

One day it hit him, "This is the way my father cared for me and I treated him the same way the pigs are treating me." The prodigal had a view from his father's eyes. It became the revelation that drew his heart back to his father.

When I was a young boy I would visit Uncle Lewis, who had a farm. He had to be careful that the pigs would not knock him down as he was pouring the food from the large pails into the trough. He would quietly walk to the trough, fill it, and then call them loudly, as he was quickly moving out of the way. They would immediately sprint towards the trough trying to outrun the other pigs as soon as they heard his call. When eating, pigs enter into a mild frenzy. It always seemed as if there was one more piglet than the length of the trough where they were devouring their food.

The one lone pig would look for a place to get to the trough and there was no room. The piglet would take one step back and ram forward using his nose and body as a wedge, and one piglet would literally be knocked off the end of the trough, three to five piglets away from the ramming piglet! This displaced piglet would immediately start squealing as his unfinished meal was being devoured by others. The piglet would run around the trough looking for the easiest place to ram back to the trough, displacing another piglet on the end he had just left.

This was an entertaining, endless cycle until the food was gone. Then all the pigs returned to roll in the mud or lay in the shade with no interest in my uncle. Pigs do not typically bond with people like other animals that are normally chosen as pets—yet they are arguably just as smart. They are simply—for a lack of a more descriptive word—pigs!

When we use the father to simply access our inheritance without a meaningful relationship, it opens the door for the enemy to steal what we have gained. Sometimes, He will allow us to increase without any meaningful relationships—a cursed success. Reaching goals of great success will reveal the emptiness of a life apart from Our Father.

Coming To Ourselves

But when he came to himself, he said, "How many of my father's hired servants have bread enough and to spare, and I perish with hunger! I will arise and go to my father, and will say to him, 'Father, I have sinned against heaven and before you, and I am no longer worthy to be called your son. Make me like one of your hired servants.' (Luke 15:17-19 NKJV)

Before the son could return to his father, he had to come to himself. Up to this point, he was thinking of what everyone else had done to put him in this situation. It was his father's fault for not sending help. The older brother hated him. The friends that he entertained should have given him a place to stay; he was so good to them.

The citizen was selfish and cruel. He did not pay him the proper wages, nor offer him the food he gave the pigs—and the pigs left him nothing! The president should have a program to feed people during famines. God is harsh. He could stop this famine. Why didn't He?

Finally he came to himself—*this is a long trip for many people*. He confessed that he had sinned against Heaven. Even though we see his wild living, we do not know the anger he had against God. In the story we see no account of his mother. I believe she was dead. Two children was a very small family in that day. Obviously I cannot prove this. Nevertheless, I do believe this prodigal was angry at God about something.

Most people that rebel against God have an issue of disappointment, hurt and anger. The enemy accuses God as the source of that hurt, and if they agree it produces a rebellious spirit.

Rebellion always points the finger at others since it is linked to the accuser. Rebellion is the opposite of conviction. Rebellion makes it very difficult to see the changes that we need to make to enter into our full blessing. It is a strategy of hell to intercept and stop Heaven from moving through us as sons on this earth.

Conviction is the pivotal point of all change. Conviction is the inner strength that comes from truth that powers our life past existing circumstances. Conviction will bring personal repentance and societal reformation.

The prodigal said, "I will arise." To move from a famine season into a new season of your life, you must arise. You cannot arise to a higher place without choosing to return to the Father or coming closer to the Father. He is the source of your new season.

The closer you are to the Father, the more elevated your next season will be. The Father has a higher level for you to live. You will access it by Him and through Him. We must move where we have chosen to live and live where He has chosen to bless us—living as sons in His presence.

Arise from where you are living and enter a new season. Declare—speak the transition—to activate the shift. *"I am arising—returning to my Father!"*

Separated Living

We can use what Father God has freely given us to build a life apart from him—while still calling Him Father. The prodigal lived apart from his father before he left his father.

As we are growing up, we have distinctive attitudes towards our parents at different stages. As we individuate in our identity, we naturally try to find our identity apart from our parents.

Elementary children run excitedly from school to greet their parents with hugs and shouts. It is very easy to discern their parents, as they each respond with open joy to each other. As those same children grow older, they often do not want their parents to pick them up at their high school. Running, shouting, and hugging are totally out of the question as the insecure teenagers now have a greater desire to be accepted by their equally insecure friends, rather than be connected to their parents.

Often teenagers will slide down in the car seat or look away from their friends as they ride away from the school with their parents. Parents are not cool when we are in high school. We are trying to establish our identity. We do not want to be seen as those elementary kids. We are able to take care of ourselves—even though we live in their house, and eat their food as they pay the bills.

This demonic spirit that tries to separate teenagers from their parents also attempts to enter between us and Father God. Most teenagers do not understand that a great relationship with their parents will actually strengthen every other meaningful relationship. If a teenager does not want their parents to meet their friends, they probably should not be their friends.

The son was reflecting on the hired servants of his father and how he treated them, as he fed the pigs. The prodigal could see his father's goodness compared to the citizen to whom he had joined himself. Can we see Our Father's goodness? It is not easy because the enemy is desperately trying to block our view.

If we refuse to connect to Father God, we will join ourselves to someone who will undervalue our lives. Father God will use them to drive us back to Him.

Revelation came to the prodigal as he was perishing with hunger. There is a hunger that is inside of each son who lives apart from the father. It's a desire in each heart that can only be filled by Our Father.

The son realized before Heaven that he had failed as a son. His repentance was based on that revelation—not that he had wasted his inheritance. The prodigal had a revelation of himself as he was living with the pigs.

"I am no longer worthy to be called your son." This statement reveals several truths. The prodigal realized that he was still a son. He was now judging his life decisions by the fact that he was a son, not a sinner nor a servant. This is key in his restoration to his father. The prodigal can always go home because he is still a _____. Did you guess the right answer? Son. A perfect orphan can never go home.

When you see your life as a son to Our Father you will have set a unique standard for your life that others cannot comprehend. It will bring a quality to your decisions and actions that have tremendous significance to your life and everything around you. If you see yourself only as a servant or a sinner saved by grace, it can set a different standard by which you judge your life and set lower expectations for your future.

The prodigal knew he was not worthy. Why? He finally comprehended how his father had treated him and how he had treated his father. He weighed his father's goodness against his selfishness. He was a son who acted as a slave.

Returning To Our Father

*And he arose and came to his father. But when
he was still a great way off, his father saw him
and had compassion, and ran and fell on his
neck and kissed him.* (Luke 15:20 NKJV)

Every prodigal must arise from where they have chosen
to live and return to the where his father lives. This decision
must be reached by the prodigal, not by the father who is
waiting.

The son was walking back to his father. The father was
running towards his son. The father's unrelenting passion to
be with his son was displayed *before* the prodigal had the
chance to repent to him.

The father saw the son—before the son saw the father.
Fathers have the greatest vision for the relationships.

It is important to recognize that *the prodigal was not
coming home, but rather he was coming to his father.* The
older son was at home, but had *never come to his father.*

The prodigal was now seeing his father in a different light
and it was shifting and healing his broken life. We must have
a revelation of Our Father God before we can truly come to
Him. Then we will arise from the place where we have been
dying—to live with Him.

The father did not pursue the son while he was in riotous
living, but he believed and waited for better day.

No Longer Worthy

And the son said to him, "Father, I have sinned against heaven and in your sight, and am no longer worthy to be called your son." (Luke 15:21 NKJV)

The son came home resigned to be a servant in his father's house—he knew he had been an unworthy son. The elder son was unaware that he was the same—unworthy. The father poured his great love over his son as he ran towards him—before words could even be spoken.

The father's *love was given before repentance, but restoration was given after repentance*. The father needed no reason to love the prodigal—except that he was *his son*. You are his son!

As the father ran towards the son, the son had to be thinking of when he ran from his father. Every step of the father brought a deeper revelation of how much he was always loved.

The famine returned the son to his father, but his father's unrestrained love brought him to total restoration.

The son first repented of his sin against Heaven. This speaks of his issues against Father God. Next was his repentance to his natural father. We cannot truly honor our natural fathers if we do not honor Father God. We also cannot honor Father God while hating our natural father.

To sin against our natural fathers is to sin against Heaven as well. Why? The scriptures teach us to honor those that are in authority and to pray for them. How much more should we do the same for our natural fathers?

The prodigal had not seen his father for a long time. The memory of his father's love toward his servants started shifting the prodigal's hard heart. He started to see his rebellion and selfishness. It is easier to see our broken relationship with Our Father in our sins than in our goodness. Yet, it is still difficult to believe He would restore us as a son after our rejection of Him.

Some of us have never met our natural father, so we have many judgments against them, as well as fear of a father—while also deeply desiring one. This fear can keep us from honoring or relating correctly to the "fathers" in our lives. We can unconsciously "father" ourselves to survive—especially in wounded areas of our heart—but it will never allow us to thrive. We can live with diluted and distorted vision of what a father truly is—believing it is accurate.

My father complimented me as young man, telling me that I was the only one of his children that he never had to worry about or help through difficult situations. Years later I realized that it actually blocked my ability to receive from Father God in many areas as I pursued being more responsible. It also translated in my subconscious that he actually cared less about me—it also made me very tired in my spirit.

If we do not honor God *as our Father,* it will not go well with us. If we honor him as our Savior, we are saved. If we honor him as our Healer, we are healed. If we honor him as the Prince of Peace, we will have peace. If we believe He cares for us, we will not take on false responsibility.

But when we honor Him as our Father, *things* go well for us. *"Things"* carry a large level of inclusions. We could be saved and healed, but many *things* might not be going well for us. The honor of the Father and "fathers" keeps an anointing on *things* in our lives.

We often perceive a father as one who is only needed to help us through our early years of development because of our natural limitations and lack of funding. As we gain our abilities to take care of ourselves, we mix our new found abilities with a spirit of independence. Therefore we do not receive the authority from our Father that belongs to sons. The greatest authority belongs to those who rest and operate from His perfect love.

Selfishness and self-centeredness obliterates our identity as sons. Jesus said that the Father never left Him, because

He lived to please His Father. Selfishness and self-centeredness is nothing less than the spirit of Lucifer. Living to please yourself is like chasing the wind in a hurricane.

The Best Robe

But the father said to his servants, "Bring[1] out the best robe and put it on him, and put a ring on his hand and sandals on his feet." (Luke 15:22 NKJV)

Notice that the father interrupted the son before he even had the chance to ask his father to make him like one of His servants. Many returning prodigals—which we all are—have ignored the father's voice and insisted that we live as servants in our father's house. We feel we do not deserve to be sons anymore—missing the desire and the design of their father— living under our own judgment instead of the father's justice of love and mercy. We are now fathering ourselves versus allowing Him to be Our Father—downgrading ourselves to live as servants, if not slaves.

It takes a father to reveal a son. The father's voice reaffirmed the prodigal's sonship before he could state that he had resigned in his heart from that favored position. The prodigal chose to believe his father over his assessment and entered into his father's celebration of him as a son. Please enter your

Father's celebration as a favored son. Believe Him—over your self-rejection.

The father did not run towards his son with the robe, ring and sandals—he simply brought himself. The father presented himself as the prize, not that which he would restore to his son. The son needed to focus on his father. The father could not restore what the son had formerly valued, until the son valued what he had previously despised—his father.

The son's repentance changed his entire assessment of everything around him. Until the value of the father was established above everything else, he was unable to truly live as a son with an inheritance.

The prodigal was lost in his rebellion, and the older son was lost in his goodness. *Sons should be lost in their father.* Jesus stood where His Father stood and saw what His Father saw. He spoke what His Father spoke and did what He saw His Father doing. Life on earth was designed to be The Father and The Son and sons' business.

Jesus said, "If you've seen me, you have seen the Father." Jesus was the perfect, full reflection of Our Father. We are partial reflections of Our Father to the world.

There will be a church that is to be filled with the same glory that Jesus carried! Without that glory, we will never be able to fulfill what Our Father desires. The glory that Jesus received from His Father was anointing, love, wisdom, miracles, and joy. This list continues with the character and abilities of Our Father.

The father gave his son the best coat, a ring, and sandals. The coat of favor means you will be received by others. The ring of authority anoints you to rule again. Sandals give you the ability to do business.

Joseph received favor and authority to guide the most powerful nation on the earth during his life through a famine. It benefited the entire world, as well as God's people. It's not wrong to help the world Our Father loves.

Many Christians are content with just the coat of favor— being received by others. We need more "Joseph" Christians who will wear the ring of authority to help others.

Moses removed his sandals to honor Father God as the greater at the burning bush. Sandals were often used to establish covenants—and Father God established one with Moses before he faced Pharaoh. Covenants break bondage and release blessings.

Joseph was sent by Father God to bring Israel into Egypt to preserve them through the famine. Then He sent Moses to bring them out of Egypt to worship the Father, and to take them into the Promised Land that Abraham had received by covenant. The Father's covenant enlarged Israel in Egypt and delivered them in the fullness of time. The Father's covenant will bring us into our promised land.

Sandals were needed to flourish in that day. If someone did not have sandals, they were typically destitute or a slave. The prodigal son was both. A slave mentality in a son cannot do covenant business in the gates of the city. The Father is handing out sandals. Wear them in the gates of your city and nation, and the nations. Walk as a son on this earth—it honors and pleases Our Father. It creates a much more enjoyable life for us and those around us.

Jesus turned to the rich young ruler and told him to sell everything he had and follow Him. There were two issues Jesus was addressing. The first one was not the riches that the young ruler had, but rather the riches that had him. Jesus never asks for less than all. He especially focuses on *what has you.*

The young man was a ruler—quite an accomplishment for a young man. This young man had to give up *being a ruler over others* to become a son. It is difficult to give up ruling our own lives. Jesus gave the rich young ruler an amazing invitation to break free of what had him, into what Father God had for him, but he refused. Jesus did not speak this to every wealthy person—only to him.

Every son must see His Father as everything before Father God can entrust that son with the best of Heaven.

The father directed to his servants to re-mantle his son. The same servants that attended the father were now attending his son, reminding the prodigal that he was not a servant— but a son.

It was not just a robe, but it was the best robe. It speaks of the favor of Joseph and a symbol of the father's great love for his son. There is a robe of favor waiting for sons who come to their father.

Your best robe is not in your closet—it is in your Father's house. *It's not your robe—it's His robe!*

When you return to The Father he will use many of other servants to dress you in honor, authority and influence—just as the enemy uses others to strip you of it.

The Celebration

"And bring the fatted calf here and kill it, and let us eat and be merry, for this my son was dead and is alive again; he was lost and is found." And they began to be merry. (Luke 15:23, 24 NKJV)

The fatted calf was saved for very special guests and special occasions—both applied this day! The father wanted to celebrate his son who was dead. We must understand that life apart from the father is death. The closer we come to Our Father, the more alive we become as His life flows through our life.

The prodigal was lost. The father knew where he was and what he was doing—as the older brother did. If we forget Our Father, we will lose our identity and it will be impossible for us to know where we are going. When he "came to himself" he realized that he was an unworthy son. That assessment factored in his father and his identity as a son. When we remember Our Father—direction is restored. The first step is to return to Our Father.

The sacrifice the Father required, we needed. We needed it to live with ourselves. It gave us a new life, a new identity. We needed it to live in His presence. It released the glory of the Father into our lives as we became sons to Him. Once we are sons we can still drift from Our Father, needing restoration and celebration again.

What you have been saved for is greater than what you have been saved from. Our amazing destiny is preceded and empowered by a great salvation. All the angels in heaven rejoice when one soul is saved. There is constant rejoicing in heaven as more are saved around the world than there are minutes in an hour. He who saved you is over-committed to keeping you—and restoring you.

The prodigal went from an unworthy son to "my son." The first title was derived from the son and his view of his life. The second title is derived from the father and his love for his son. We must be willing to agree with Our Father's view of our life.

You are my hiding place; You shall preserve me from trouble; You shall surround me with songs of deliverance.[17] The Lord your God in your midst, The Mighty One, will save;

---

[17] *The New King James Version.* (1982). (Ps 32:7). Nashville: Thomas Nelson.

He will rejoice over you with gladness, He will quiet you with His love, He will rejoice over you with singing."[18]

Our Father is singing over us, rejoicing over us. That is simply amazing. He is also surrounding us with songs of deliverance. He is singing songs of deliverance that defeat the enemy and restore our heart. We are worshiping Him and He is celebrating us. It produces a mighty victory when His songs of deliverance intersect with our worship.

Our Father did not tell the angels to sing over us, He is singing over us. Our worship connects to His song of deliverance. It releases heaven into the earth realm. It brings His strength into our lives and situations. Is it possible that Father God was singing songs of deliverance over David as he was running towards Goliath and running from King Saul?

Can you hear His celebration over you as you are worshipping Him? It brings more than healing—it brings hope and fresh vision! Our worship of Our Father brings His presence and releasing His power through our lives. His celebration over us shifts our identity. It reinforces the relationship we have with Him and takes it to the next level.

The celebration of the Father shifts our life into new seasons and greater purposes. They increase vision and release new authority. The Father's celebration breaks off specific limitations of the past season that would block the assignments of the next season.

---

[18] *The New King James Version*. (1982). (Zep 3:17). Nashville: Thomas Nelson.

We do not look for what we do not believe exists. We need to believe the scriptures, we just read. We need to visualize the Father rejoicing over us. He not only loves us, He is excited about us. We know the ultimate celebration we will all enjoy around His throne. When we experience a special time or a unique victory in our lives, we need to worship Him. Then we need to listen. Can we hear Him rejoicing over us? Close your eyes. Open your heart to the Father's celebration. Raise your awareness—He is rejoicing over you.

The forgiveness of the father brought a cleansing to the prodigal, but the celebration of the father restored his identity! "He is *my son*." We must enter into the celebration by our Father for our identity to be restored and empowered.

We must accept His invitation to enter into His celebrations. We must attend the celebrations that He has for our brothers, whether they are victory or restoration celebrations, as well as those He has planned for us.

The prodigal son could have refused his father's celebration based on the guilt and shame of the past the enemy was trying to lock around his heart. The love of his father was a chain breaker. He stepped into his father's heart, out of his past and into his future.

When we live in His celebration it creates a paradigm shift in us that is multi-dimensional. Celebrations are incredible events that help establish our identity and value. The younger son never saw himself as the prodigal after the father's celebration—nor did the father.

As the father and his son were celebrating together, the son entered into the spirit of his father. This qualified him to receive his inheritance for his restored season. Our Father has deep pockets. As we worship Our Father, we receive Him. That allows His greatness and abilities to flow through us— it's a game changer.

Our worship is what we give to Him. He receives it. He rejoices over us. *Receive it.* We understand how important our worship is to our life as a believer. We benefit from the scriptural worship He has called us to give. Everything Our Father does has great significance and purpose.

We pray to Father God and we expect Him to direct us, speak to us and comfort us. He responds to our interaction with Him. Why we would expect Him to be non-responsive when we worship Him? He is a good Father who responds to the worship of His children with songs of rejoicing over them.

We are starting to understand the benefits of His rejoicing over us. It breaks the fatherless spirit that the enemy has released over the earth. It emboldens the Father's sons and daughters to run towards Goliath like David, shattering the spirit of fear and insignificance. It delivers us from the hand of the enemy. It is preparing Christians to enter into the greatest anointing the earth has ever seen.

Declare: I worship Father God and He rejoices over me. He receives my worship and I receive His rejoicing. I know that I am favored by the Father. He is singing songs of deliverance over me. It is breaking every negative attack of the enemy and releasing fresh glory into my life. You're awesome, Father! I love You!

Listen: *What do you hear Him saying as He rejoices over you? Write it down.*

The Angry Refusal

Now his older son was in the field. And as he came and drew near to the house, he heard music and dancing. So he called one of the servants and asked what these things meant. And he said to him, "Your brother has come, and because he has received him safe and sound, your father has killed the fatted calf." But he was angry and would not go in. (Luke 15:25-28 NKJV)

The older son could not enter the celebration because he was standing in judgment of his father. The father was aware of his eldest son's attitude. The prodigal needed to come from a foreign land to his father, and the older brother needed to come from the fields to his father.

For the son in a foreign land—the father waited outside the house. For the son in his fields—the father was waited inside his house as the celebration started. He is waiting and looking for his lost sons in appropriate places every time.

The prodigal left the *famine and pigs* to come to his father. The oldest son needed to leave *his fields and his servants* to come to his father. The prodigal had to leave his badness; the elder brother had to leave his goodness.

The problem of the older son is revealed in these verses. As he drew near to the house, he stopped and asked one of the servants what was happening. He did not see the house as his home. He stopped outside of the house like a stranger, instead of coming in like a son.

He did not communicate with his Father, but chose to inquire of *one of the servants* to find out what was happening in his father's house. He knew less than a servant, even though he was a son—a lost son. We can lose our keys to a vehicle on a trip or we can lose them in our house. Lost is lost.

The oldest became so dedicated to the fields that at some point he disconnected from his father. This son did not understand his father's desire for him or his brother. He could not comprehend his father's love towards his rebellious brother— because he did not possess his father's heart.

He worked in his father's fields, resenting his father and his brother. He judged his father as a demanding master. He treated his brother according to his judgments against his father. Our view of our Father will determine how we treat our brothers. If we see Him as a good Father, we will treat others from His goodness.

Many of us might be inclined to agree with the older son's resistance to this seemingly premature celebration. His deep resentment towards his father is revealed at his father's invitation to celebrate his wayward brother's return.

The responsible brother's judgment of his irresponsible brother and his astounding burning resentment towards his father—turned into an outright refusal to his father's request—rebellion. The elder son had no honor for his father. He had rejected his father. His did not agree with his father's ways, nor did he care to learn them.

Therefore his father came out and pleaded with him. So he answered and said to his father, "Lo, these many years I have been serving you; I never transgressed your commandment at any time; and yet you never gave me a young goat, that I might make merry with my friends. But as soon as this son of yours came, who has devoured your livelihood with harlots, you killed the fatted calf for him." (Luke 15:28-30 NKJV)

The father came out, searching for his other lost son. Either the father looked around and saw he was missing, or a servant informed the father of his older son's angry response. The father was waiting for him in his house—a place his son did not desire—he loved the fields.

The father had plenty of servants to work in the fields. He wanted his sons living in his house with him—sons who would walk in His authority doing His will in His fields.

We see the heart of the Father as he is pleading with his oldest son. The son's response to his father reveals an ungodly ugly attitude—just like the Pharisees that were listening to Jesus.

We see the anger of the oldest son burning against his father, not his brother. He informs his father of the many years he had been serving him—but he was not serving his father—he was serving his inheritance. If we focus on *what* is ours—we lose *who* is ours.

One translation uses the word "slaved" instead of "serving." He viewed his father as a slave master—so he worked and thought as a slave. Therefore, he expected his father to treat his younger brother as a runaway slave—punishing him, and then putting him back to work in the fields. A celebration for the prodigal was unthinkable!

The eldest son never transgressed one of his father's commands—but he was not like him. He never loved him or approached him as his father. He loved his spotless record. He loved himself. He saw himself superior to his younger brother and wiser than his father. If his wayward brother was being celebrated—why had his father never celebrated him, the son who had not left home? Jealousy was affecting the older brother. It always deceives and drains the anointing.

The oldest brother did not want his father to receive his younger brother. Based on his past record, the younger brother was unworthy. This reveals that the older brother's relationship with his father was based on his clean record and hard labor—correct thinking for an employee, but very strange for a son. The elder son was willing to labor, but he refused a life with his father.

The older son was slaving in the midst of his inheritance. His view of his father was twisted by the enemy. Our perception of Father God has dramatic impact on our identity and activity—affecting our entire destiny.

He was trying to earn what he had already acquired—therefore he could not receive it. No one can earn what is given. Receiving is simplistic in nature, but it's not easy. The older son would not go into his father's house even after the father entreated him—but the prodigal did.

The older brother was celebrating his life and the work of his hands, not his father. He was critical of his father and that "son of yours." Until we see other "prodigals" as our brothers, we will never have a vision to restore them as sons to our Father.

The older brother judged his father the day he gave his younger brother his inheritance—blocking his ability to receive his inheritance that had been divided to him that same day as well! If the elder brother would have entered into his father's celebration of his prodigal brother, it would have shattered his judgments against his father. It would have allowed him to receive his inheritance from his father that was granted years ago.

The obedient brother was upset that his father had never had given him a goat to celebrate with his friends. The fatted calf was reserved for the father's celebrations of his sons in his house—not for sons slaving as foreigners in the fields.

The prodigal was celebrating his relationship with his father in this party. The oldest brother did not want to celebrate his father's restoration of his younger brother, so he remained unrestored. He still preferred a party with his friends—not his family.

A reward teaches a person to do it again, in the same spirit and manner. God, Our Father, therefore cannot celebrate our dysfunctional approaches to Him lest we reason that we should live there forever. He is still celebrating us as His sons and daughters—but it is difficult to hear it from our house. It is easily heard when we live in His house—in His presence.

The oldest son lived in his good works outside the father's house while the prodigal entered his father's goodness and greatness, choosing to live in his father's celebration. Until we live in our father's celebration of our life, we will not have full access to our destiny or the abilities He gave us.

Always With Me

And he said to him, "Son, you are always with me, and all that I have is yours. It was right that we should make merry and be glad, for your brother was dead and is alive again, and was lost and is found." (Luke 15:31, 32 NKJV)

The older son was always with his father—yet he was totally disconnected. We must break the patterns that are established in our childhood with our fathers that are considered normal, but are truly dysfunctional. Years ago, I heard a study was done that calculated the average conversation between a child and a parent in one day. It was a painful figure—nine and seventeen minutes for a father and mother respectively.

Children can be in their father's presence, yet there is little communication. The interaction of parents and children is often based in the tasks assigned to children or what the parents desired them to accomplish. Children's normal needs are covered by parents, but with limited communication. Rarely did our parents ever sit down and just talk with us about their life or ours.

We bring this pattern into our relationship with Our Father. It would not be difficult to believe that many believers would only communicate with Father God about the same amount of time each day that our parents did with us and their parents did with them—very little. We are breaking the time pattern the enemy has set over our lives concerning fathers.

I am with you always, even to the end of the age." [19] *For He Himself has said, "I will never leave you nor forsake you."* [20]

As we reflect on these two scriptures, we realize that Our Father is always with us—but are we enjoying His presence? Are we enjoying Him? Are we communicating with Him in moments during each day, or are we waiting for Sunday morning corporate gathering or our personal morning devotions to tell Him that we love Him.

The Bible instructs not to neglect the gathering of the saints. There is something powerful that occurs when we come together with other sons and daughters to honor Our Father. A birthday party for our natural father would not be

---

[19] *The New King James Version.* (1982). (Mt 28:20). Nashville: Thomas Nelson.

[20] *The New King James Version.* (1982). (Heb 13:5). Nashville: Thomas Nelson.

the same if one of his children refused to come—versus they could not make it this time. It would be quite hurtful to the other siblings and disappointing to the father.

Yet the father desires the personal attention and love of each child that can only happen when they are alone together. The birthday party would not replace the intimate time he expects and desires with each child individually. The lack of personal time together would actually diminish the joy and the celebration of his birthday gathering.

He is always with us! Capture a moment with Him—right now! Turn your heart towards Him and talk with Him in a very personal way. He said He would never leave us—*but what are we doing with that personal opportunity?* Let's not just ask for His help. He's not there for the next project—He's there for you. It's time to move closer to Him—closer than you've ever been before.

Get to know Him. Communicate—build the relationship, not a strategy. A man was weeping as he told me that his lifetime friend had passed away. He started listing everything they had done together as children, young men and in their adulthood—many moments in every season of life.

They had built a strong friendship based on open communication that was frequent—they were very connected throughout their entire lives and knew each other well. How would our friends feel if they were always with us and we gave them the same amount of attention we give Our Father each day? This is not to condemn anyone, but rather to make us aware with a reality we can all understand.

Our Father does not want to be ignored. Take advantage of the fact that He is always with you—talk to Him. Love Him. Listen to His heart. He will fill your life with His presence and direct your path as you *acknowledge Him in all your ways*. Seize moments throughout each day to fellowship with your Father. His presence will create peace and momentum in each day. He is always with us. Factor that advantage in everything you do! Enjoy Him in the journey. Build a deeper friendship.

He is with us to give us the opportunity to take the relationship to the next level. When He lifts us up into a new season, let's embrace Him—fixing our eyes and our heart on Him before gazing at the promised land of our new season. Priority and passion for Him are required in His kingdom for very practical reasons—it safeguards our hearts from making idols out of His blessings and our purpose.

When a grandparent buys a toy for their grandchild, they do their best to find a toy their child will truly love. They expect to see joy and excitement on the face of that little one as they receive the toy, playing with it. What the grandparent wants is lots of hugs and lots of love. It would be very unhealthy for that grandchild to hug the toy and say how much they loved the toy—totally ignoring the grandparent.

The time between the gift received and the child hugging and loving the grandparent will reveal the level of closeness in the relationship. What grandparent would not be overjoyed if the child ran past the gift and tackled them with hugs and kisses? Let's "overjoy" our Father!

Let's run past our inheritance and embrace Our Father, but don't forget He brought something very special—just for us! He picked it out to make us happy! He is an awesome Father! Don't forget your inheritance—He didn't.

My father and mother are both in Heaven—I miss them. I would often take time to stop by to see them as I was going to the church office or running an errand, even after a very hurtful event had transpired from a decision they made. I had a great relationship with my parents, but I still had to build past a hurt. I believe that everyone has that challenge in the best of relationships.

Taking advantage of my parent's presence while they were on this earth positioned me to rest in the love in our relationship versus that hurtful past event. The more time you invest in any relationship, the greater value it will have. There are a few times in life where an unhealthy attitude in others requires a temporary step back to allow Father God to work without our interference or help.

The father came outside his house to bring His oldest son in with him. The oldest son never left home and slept every night in that house. He never lived with his father— he just lived in a room in his father's house. If we are not comfortable in our Father's presence, we will slave in the fields instead of having dominion in them. When Adam fell from dominion, he hid from his Father in his Father's garden. We must overcome Adam's syndrome. We can even hide in His house.

This father had to go out of his house to meet both of his sons. It is the job description of fathers. He gave the prodigal who repented mercy and honor. The father entreated the older brother to join him in celebrating his repentant brother. The father knew it would break his self-righteousness and lack of mercy.

The celebration the older son really needed in his life was not the one he desired with his friends, but the celebration his father gave for the younger brother. It would have been a life-changing event for him—but he declined. When we enter into the celebrations Father God chooses for His restored sons and daughters, we keep or acquire His heart. He has already chosen celebrations for others that will change their lives—and ours as well, if we attend.

A New Creation—A "son" Of God

Therefore, if anyone is in Christ, he is a new creation; old things have passed away; behold, all things have become new. [21]

This is a powerful scripture utilized by many believers—but what does it mean? The identity of being a sinner has

---

[21] *The New King James Version.* (1982). (2 Co 5:17). Nashville: Thomas Nelson.

passed away and Father God has made us a new creation—His sons! The father never called his son a prodigal—he only referred to him as *my son!*

It is important to realize that this is not an exclusive relationship for a few elite believers, but an open invitation to all who call on the name of Jesus Christ.

I am a son to Lawrence Mast because he birthed me—my mother delivered me. It's that simple. I am a son to Father God because He rebirthed me through the blood of Jesus Christ—I was born again—birthed again.

Father God created and formed me in my mother's womb. He knew me and called me before I was born—He is my Creator—desiring to become my Father! The first Adam walked us away from the Father God. The last Adam walked us back to Father God.

Father God created the first Adam as a son to Him. Father God sent the last Adam, Jesus Christ—The Son of God, so we could be rebirthed as sons to Him. We are now a new creation! We were not made angels or spirit beings. What did that new creation accomplish? It took away our identity as sinners and birthed us as children to Father God. We are sons because He rebirthed us through Christ! It's that simple.

But as many as received Him, to them He gave the right to become children of God, to those who believe in His name:

who were born, not of blood, nor of the will of the flesh, nor of the will of man, but of God.[22]

We were born again as children of God by the will of God. It is God's will that we live as His children with Him. We have the right to become children of God. The right to become the children of God must be reinforced with a relationship, communication, understanding and passionate pursuit to possess the fullness of it. We must receive God's Son to become a son. It takes The Son to restore a son.

As believers who have been rebirthed, we must speak what He has created us to be to Him. We must break off negative words that have altered our identity—negative words that will bind us until they are removed and replaced with truth. Let this declaration shift your thinking.

I am a child of Father God. When I live as a child of God, I am in His perfect will. He is my Father. He desires my presence. I love my Father's presence! My Father God gave me the right to live on this earth as His child! I will live in my Father's love.

My loving Father is watching over me and everything that concerns me. He will care for me as His child. He is always with me. He has an inheritance for me. As His child, I am favored and have privileged access to Him. Because My Father is for me, who can be against me? All things

---

[22] *The New King James Version.* (1982). (Jn 1:12–13). Nashville: Thomas Nelson.

concerning my life are possible because the God I serve is also my Father.

We must come to Father God as children if we are ever to become sons. The implicit trust and innocent faith that emanates from children is the foundation required to grow into mature sons. Sons can only come from children. No matter how old you are when you are born again, you must become a child of God. That childlike element of faith will keep every believer young at heart all the days of their life.

The child in us dreams easier than the adult in us. The adult has better plans to accomplish the dream. The teenager in us will dare to do it. The adult in us will pick when to do it. The child in us simply believes. Each component is very important.

Any wounding in a particular developmental season of our life that is not healed can steal the strength of that season or cause us to overuse the other seasons. Father God uses these different seasons in our life to develop multi-dimensional strengths in our heart and spirit to empower our destiny with victory.

If we are healed in every area of our life, we have greater authority and creativity. We will also be able to flow with Father God naturally and supernaturally. Then Satan will have no major place to block the acceleration and expansion of our destiny.

Behold what manner of love the Father has bestowed on us, that we should be called children of God! [23]

Names we give to those around us reflect the relationship and our love for them. I have many friends, but only four people on this earth are my children. When I refer to someone else as one of my "children," there is something extra special about that relationship.

His great love has called us His children. If we do not receive that identity, we are rejecting Father God's love for us. Do we comprehend the level of love that Father God has for us to call us His children? Let it sink in very deep—past the rejection and abandonment this world has placed on us.

Friends have said to my wife and me, "We are your children." What are they implying? *"You have become a father and a mother to us—please continue to deepen that trust and intimate relationship. Don't just treat me like a close friend, treat me like a son—like a daughter."*

What is the difference? There is a high level of personal interest and commitment that is given to children by a father. He takes greater responsibility from their birth to the end of his life. His children, while babies, live in his house totally protected with full provision and tender care. Fathers are committed to maturing their sons and developing their full potential so the sons can become fathers to others.

---

[23] *The New King James Version*. (1982). (1 Jn 3:1). Nashville: Thomas Nelson.

There is also a realm of discipline—training and teaching. It is a tedious process required to bring out the gifts that are within their child—without crushing their spirit, inviting laziness or rebellion. We need to utilize Our Father's wisdom and love to parent others. It is sweet and sweat to be a great parent—both naturally and spiritually.

Father God is committed to you and the greatness He put inside of you from your birth. It takes a father to reveal and mature the greatness in his son. If your natural father is not there, Father God will send you fathers and godly examples to impact your life.

Eventually all of us must come to Our Father—to be fathered. He is our Eternal Father. He is our Everlasting Father. He will always be Our Father—on earth and in Heaven—now and throughout eternity. Start enjoying it now.

Don't allow the hurts or issues from your natural parents keep you from that favored and privileged relationship. He calls you His child. You will always be His.

Quiet Talk

Let the words of my mouth and the meditation of my heart be acceptable in Your sight, O LORD, my strength and my Redeemer.[24]

---

[24] *The New King James Version.* (1982). (Ps 19:14). Nashville: Thomas Nelson.

Asking should arise from a trusted relationship with Father God that produces confident expectation. An essential key to personal growth and success is your *"quiet talk."* It is a phrase I use to describe my ongoing fellowship with Father God throughout my daily life.

It is a form of communication/meditation where I enter and stay in the Father's presence. It involves my heart, my soul, my mind and my strength to love Him.

I thank Him for always being with me. It increases my awareness that my Father is always with me. It becomes the foundation for building an enduring endearing relationship by actively sharing moments of my life with Him. It is becoming more natural to involve Him in every part of my day by seizing moments of conversation with Him. I invite Him into my day—into my heart—into my life with "quiet talk."

Our heart is where we keep our passion and priority alive. Seek Him with all of your heart right now through your quiet talk with Him.

Father, I turn my heart towards You. My love is focused on You this very moment. There is none other like You. I worship You. Thank you for your presence that surrounds me.

I desire You above all. You are my life. You've been so good to me. You brought me through difficult places—into sweet places. Thank You for not allowing the enemy's plans in that situation to destroy me. You are a wall of fire around me. I love You. Your wisdom is amazing. Your power is earth shaking.

You dug me out of situations where I was stuck. Your presence is everything to me. I place You first in my thoughts. Be a part of what I am doing today. Please come closer. I want to go deeper with You. I want You.

One day I just started humming this tune in my heart to Him until I sang it out loud. "I'm getting to know you—yeah, yeah, yeah. Learning to trust you—ooh!" I have been adding more words to my quiet worship. "I've going deeper, deeper than before, I'm coming closer, I'm coming closer."

I am learning how to come into His presence in ordinary moments—a privilege of any son. I did not know how to come into my natural father's presence. He did not seem very interested in my world unless it intersected his. Perception is not always true, but it is "our truth" from which we make decisions and derive our value.

When I am in a low intensity level task such as mowing grass or driving the car—it has the potential to become an extended time for quiet talk with my Father. Those are very special quiet times with the Father for me. What I am doing is just enough to slow me down to create a place for quiet talk. If I am in a dire situation I need everything quiet—no activity whatsoever.

The scriptures talk about redeeming the time—this is an aspect of that truth. I find that one short invitation of His presence or comment from my heart to His can change my entire day. Explore! You will discover dimensions in Him that are amazing. We are sons desiring Our Father. He desires us.

We grew up trying to understand our natural fathers. Most often they did not help us in that process. Nor did our fathers try to help us understand our lives—as they were still actively pursuing their identity and place in life. Those elements gave the impression that we were not the most important thing in life to them—for some children this was probably true. That view hampers or can totally block our ability or desire to live in Father God's presence—or to believe that it is actually possible!

If what I am doing requires creative thinking, I invite my Father's presence and His intelligence into the project.

Father, I invite your presence into my day. You see what I have before me. What do You think I should do? Where should I start? Any suggestions? You made this world—I am sure that You can handle this too! Smile. Thank you for being with this son. You are so close. Your love is so amazing. My greatest joy is knowing You. I am listening. What do you have to say?

I encourage you to use what I have written above as a starting point to develop your "quiet talk." The more comfortable you are in talking with Father God, the easier it will become to have greater revelation of Him. You will discover and develop many "windows" that you can gain access to His presence—He is always with you.

And when He had sent the multitudes away, He went up on the mountain by Himself to pray. Now when evening came, He was alone there. [25]

Jesus would often draw aside to a quiet place by himself with His Father. What did Jesus' prayer life look like? The painting depicted by an artist of Jesus kneeling in Gethsemane does not capture the form of the prayer life of Jesus. Jesus's prayer life was displayed at the raising of Lazarus—open conversation.

Then they took away the stone from the place where the dead man was lying. And Jesus lifted up His eyes and said, "Father, I thank You that You have heard Me. And I know that You always hear Me, but because of the people who are standing by I said this, that they may believe that You sent Me." Now when He had said these things, He cried with a loud voice, "Lazarus, come forth!" [26]

Jesus never closed his eyes or kneeled in this prayer. He actually looked up into the heavens as He was talking to His Father as if He was standing right in front of Him. Jesus was very natural in His communication with His Father.

Many of us are very uncomfortable entering into an open conversation with Father God. We grew up obeying our fathers—never understanding them. Why would I expect

---

[25] *The New King James Version.* (1982). (Mt 14:23). Nashville: Thomas Nelson.

[26] *The New King James Version.* (1982). (Jn 11:40–43). Nashville: Thomas Nelson.

more from my Father God? Jesus lived in an open dialogue with His Father—He showed us the way to live and how to communicate with Our Father.

My father was a happy, friendly man with a shadow of depression. He reached out to many people in amazing ways. He also had a streak of anger that put fear in my heart. It was unpredictable and fearful—though it seldom occurred. It created an inner tension that made it difficult for me to rest in the presence of Father God.

It took decades for me to totally remove my father's angry voice from my spirit and mind. My childhood was filled with great memories and dark voids—like most people. As I have counseled people over thirty years, I realize that I had a better father than most people—yet it still did not erase the damage that blocked my relationship with Father God.

I did not know how to be with my natural father outside of working in his business with him. The pattern was set—I was comfortable in my father's fields, but not in his house. I do remember listening to my Dad and uncles talk about what they did as young men. They had some great stories. I didn't understand why it brought me such a great joy to listen to them. It allowed me to view my father's life—it helped to bond me to him. Yet, I did not know how to be alone with him. I wanted to have a greater relationship with him, but I didn't know how to do it when I was younger, nor did he.

My father never came to my baseball games, even though I made the all-star team. He was working night and day. What he was doing was important—I was not. These are lies the enemy develops from situations that are imperfect, but multidimensional. These are thoughts that we cannot clarify as children and they continue to cloud our minds into our adult years. We then transfer that sense of unimportance into Our Father's eyes.

The truth is that my father started his own business at a young age. He lived in the same pattern of my grandfather, who had been adopted into an Amish family with too many girls and no sons to do the farm work. My grandfather's identity as a worker transferred to my father and I was there to receive it from my father.

My father was a farmer who had a sawmill business on the side. The farm barn burnt down when I was a young child. His part-time sawmill business became the major source of income as he focused on it. I asked my mother where Dad was the first six years of my life—I had very few memories of him. She told me, "Before you woke up, he left for work, and I would put you to sleep before he returned home in those early years."

Adjustments were needed in my father's life, but it was not an indicator that he did not love me. He was running the combine in the fields when I was born in a nearby hospital. I was told he was overjoyed when he found out he had a son for his second child. Specific events recalled by others can tell you one story; the life you remember can tell you another one.

As soon as school was over, I worked in my father's lumber business from the age of twelve. This meant that I could not play basketball that I enjoyed except for one year in junior high. These are not huge issues, but the paradigm that was being created inside of me was huge.

After many years of being a dedicated Christian leader, it still was an integral part of my relationship with Father God. I was a great worker for Him, but it was difficult to believe that He wanted to spend time with me, just for me, even though I knew the scriptures said He did.

I believed that I would never really get to enjoy my life like others—I had work to do. While I enjoyed working with God, it was more difficult to believe He really enjoyed me. I was slipping towards being like the elder son as I worked in His fields. I was living my Grandfather's life with Father God—I was needed to get the work done.

If I did something outstanding, my father would tell others. If I did something wrong, he would raise his voice or yell at me. I remember the first time I ever heard my father talk about me in a positive way at the age of fourteen. I was resting in bed, trying to sleep when I overheard my father's voice come through the walls from the dining room. "Dale's such a good worker. He can do a man's work."

I remember the smile that came to my uncertain heart as I heard that affirmation. It was not all bad nor was it all good. It set a component in my heart that would take years to dismantle. I became one of God's best workers, but struggled to set in His presence as a son. No one was as smart as my oldest sister. She could do anything and everything according to my parents. This was not helpful for me to hear what they didn't tell her.

Being raised as Mennonites, we were taught that we should not make our children proud lest they fall to the enemy. Therefore, compliments were not given at a healthy rate. Lack of confidence can destroy a person's ability to succeed just as much as pride. Lack of celebration by others over our lives reduces our strength to overcome challenging situations in life. Confidence is also a great component of vision. I am very thankful for the many other truths I learned from the Mennonites, but that one was missing.

How did I defeat the lies that kept me from my Father God and my destiny? Constantly listening to His voice removed the angry voice of my father and the angry voice of others— and my angry voice against myself.

My quiet talk started as a young boy as I was lying on my back in the grass at night gazing at the stars. I would talk quietly to God from my heart as I looked into the heavens. Now I do it purposefully. It has increased the intimacy and the anointing level in my life. The more I heard His loving voice, the angry voices became silent and the thoughts they produced were eliminated.

In studies, it has been discovered that events and words that are accompanied by strong emotions shifts the memory from short-term memory to long-term memory. That is the reason why the most negative events are easily remembered decades later. The level of occurrences can be infrequent, but the penetrating destruction is overwhelming.

We cannot host the presence of Father God with angry voices still resident inside of us. Our loving Father's voice will drive out the angry voices the enemy has planted in our lives. We hear His voice in the scriptures, in prayer, in our worship and in our quiet talk.

Some refer to it as hosting the presence of God—walking in the Spirit—abiding in Him—a Christ centered life—holy living—a restored heart—a renewed mind.

Quiet talk is seizing moments through conversational meditation with Father God as we walk through each day. He is inviting you to draw closer.

As the communication in our heart with Our Father increases to overflow, we will literally speak it. Declaration is a seed that clarifies and establishes truth in our lives and circumstances. The force created and released in that declaration has tremendous impact on our hearts as we hear it with our own ears. We are doing it in, and before Our Father. We must grow in this aspect of our lives to become fruitful. It is the method Our Father used to create this world.

What we desire should be in our *quiet talk* with Our Father, as we walk through each day. We should also speak out the desired result to shift the situation or atmosphere around it. At a certain point, there comes a rest and it transfers to an attitude of expectation in our spirit and mind. The conversation is ended, but the heavens are now open. Our Father God loves to meet us in very personal and intimate ways—but our conversation must also be personal and intimate.

Asking should be connected to the vision God has placed in our hearts. It can also be connected to a personal desire that He planted in us from birth. As we continue to pursue God through our lives, there will come a day of convergence. You will wake up saying, "I was born for this!"

All I Have Is Yours

The older son's ability to receive his inheritance was linked to entering into his father's heart towards the prodigal son. If we cannot enter Father God's heart in these matters, we will never carry the fullness of His glory, nor receive our full inheritance.

The elder brother was sinking in the middle his inheritance, because he refused to connect to his father. As in the story of the father and two sons—we need to return to Father God whether we are the prodigal son or the slaving son.

The father had already brought the prodigal son into his house wearing the best coat and new ring, but he—the loving father—went out seeking his oldest son. I am sure the father had another best coat and new ring for his oldest son, but he would not join his father. Actually, he could not join the celebration until he fell into his father's arms, repenting of his self-righteousness and lack of mercy.

The father is still standing—looking at the son who had been slaving at the end of the parable. Will he change his mind and go in with the father? There is a celebration waiting for every one of us—in His house! Will we enter as sons into Our Father's celebrations He has for us? It's our time to enter into the celebration of Our Father and receive our inheritance!

The words of the father to his eldest son are astounding; *"All I have is yours."* The father was reminding his eldest son what was available to him and his father's willingness to give it to him. The elder son still would not ask his father to receive it. His judgement against his father blocked his ability to hear or believe what his father spoke.

We have a willing, generous, good Father. All He has is ours. Until this revelation becomes reality in our lives, we will never have a correct view of Our Father nor access what He has for us.

He is Your Father—live as a son! Your inheritance is His love and provision for you. Live a life backed by your Father's favor, anointing, and resources. It's His absolute pleasure to give us the Kingdom.

Declaration: *I am a privileged and favored son, loved by my Father.*

Father God, I love you and worship you with my life. I can hear you rejoicing over me. I am so thankful that your presence is always with me. I am drawing closer.

Father, I am asking you for my inheritance to fulfill the destiny that you have chosen for me. I receive it with joy. Show me Father, how to utilize it to bring you glory. You are mine and I am yours.

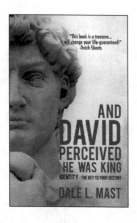

God took David from the fields where he
followed the sheep to become the ruler of
Israel. He was overlooked by his father, yet
chosen by God. He carried the dream to be
king from the day Samuel anointed him, but
he did not feel worthy to marry the king's
daughter after defeating Goliath. David experienced many amazing moments in his life,
yet he also endured many traumas. He was
the hero of Israel and then became the hunted
villain. He went from leading the armies of
Israel to being pursued by the same. When
David was anointed king in Judah, civil war
erupted. Each step that God was establishing
David's identity, the enemy was trying to
steal it. Defeating Goliath required faith, but
taking the throne required identity. It takes a
Goliath to reveal a David, and his journey to
produce a king. Faith believes what God can
do. Identity believes what God can do through
you. Let David's journey touch yours.

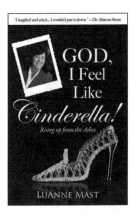

GOD, I Feel Like *Cinderella!*

Rising up from the Ashes

LUANNE MAST

Sweeping the ashes out of the fireplace at my first job as a cleaning lady, I was overwhelmed. My husband of 23 years had left me for another woman, and I was thrust into the role of a struggling single mom. At that time my mother died of cancer, my house went into foreclosure, my car was repossessed, and I was forced into unexpected bankruptcy. In frustration, I lifted my hands up to the Lord and cried out, "God, I feel like Cinderella!" He answered me right away. He said, "You are Cinderella, and I will redeem you!" I had already experienced the supernatural power of prayer, healings and miracles. I was visited by an angel and prayed for a man that was raised from the dead. So when I heard God answer me in those ashes, I knew I had to trust him like never before.

Contact Information
dalemast@aol.com
eaglefireministries.org
destinydover.org
302-674-4288